creating a presentation in powerpoint

Visual QuickProject Guide

by Tom Negrino

Peachpit
Press

Visual QuickProject Guide
Creating a Presentation in PowerPoint
Tom Negrino

Peachpit Press
1249 Eighth Street
Berkeley, CA 94710
510/524-2178
800/283-9444
510/524-2221 (fax)

Find us on the World Wide Web at: www.peachpit.com
To report errors, please send a note to errata@peachpit.com
Peachpit Press is a division of Pearson Education

Copyright © 2005 by Tom Negrino

Editor: Nancy Davis
Production Editor: Connie Jeung-Mills
Compositor: Owen Wolfson
Proofreader: Ted Waitt
Indexer: James Minkin
Cover design: The Visual Group with Aren Howell
Interior design: Elizabeth Castro
Cover photo credit: Getty One

Notice of Liability
The information in this book is distributed on an "As Is" basis, without warranty. While every precaution has been taken in the preparation of the book, neither the author nor Peachpit Press shall have any liability to any person or entity with respect to any loss or damage caused or alleged to be caused directly or indirectly by the instructions contained in this book or by the computer software and hardware products described in it.

Trademarks
Visual QuickProject Guide is a registered trademark of Peachpit Press, a division of Pearson Education.
All other trademarks are the property of their respective owners.

Throughout this book, trademarks are used. Rather than put a trademark symbol with every occurrence of a trademarked name, we state that we are using the names in an editorial fashion only and to the benefit of the trademark owner with no intention of infringement of the trademark. No such use, or the use of any trade name, is intended to convey endorsement or other affiliation with this book.

ISBN 0-321-27844-5

9 8 7 6 5 4 3 2 1

Printed and bound in the United States of America

For Dori, Sean,
and Pixel the Cat

Special Thanks to...

The Board of Directors and Staff of Access Healdsburg, community television for Healdsburg and Northern Sonoma County, CA. It's great working with you. Visit AHTV's Web site at www.ahtv.org.

My superb editor, Nancy Davis.

The book's production editor, Connie Jeung-Mills.

Thanks to Lockie Gillies, Brett Pollard, and Vince Dougherty of Wine Country Computers, www.winecomputers.com, for the use of their computers.

contents

contents

contents

introduction

The Visual QuickProject Guide that you hold in your hands offers a unique way to learn about new technologies. Instead of drowning you in theoretical possibilities and lengthy explanations, this Visual QuickProject Guide uses big, color illustrations coupled with clear, concise step-by-step instructions to show you how to complete one specific project in a matter of hours.

Our project in this book is to create a compelling and colorful presentation using Microsoft PowerPoint. We'll use either PowerPoint 2003 for Windows or PowerPoint 2004 for Macintosh. These are the latest versions, but if you haven't upgraded yet, don't fret; things will look pretty familiar if you have PowerPoint 2000 or XP for Windows or PowerPoint X for Mac.

We will create a fundraising presentation for a real non-profit organization, Access Healdsburg, which is a community television station located in Sonoma County, California. But because the presentation showcases all the basic techniques, you'll be able to use what you learn to create your own presentations, whether it be a talk for your annual sales meeting, a lecture for a class you're teaching, or a slide show for your department detailing your latest work.

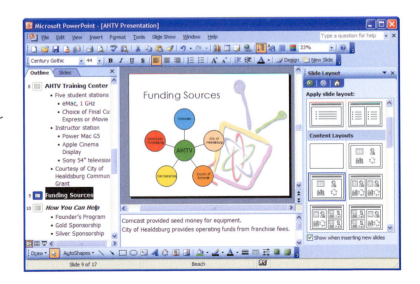

what you'll create

Write your presentation in PowerPoint's Outline View.

Apply slide layouts from the gallery.

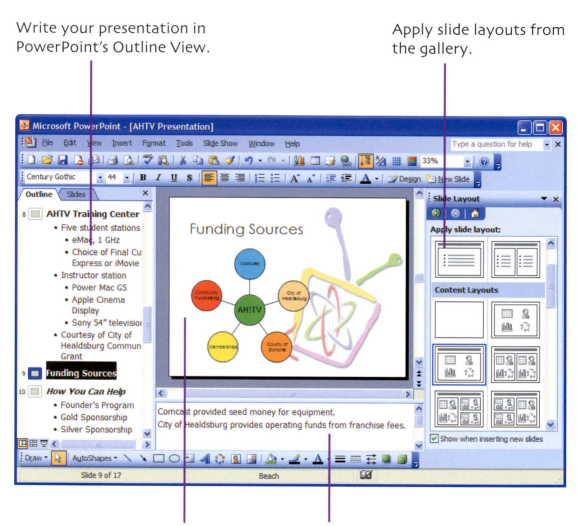

Create colorful, attractive diagrams with the Drawing toolbar to illustrate your message.

Add Speaker Notes to help keep your presentation on track when you give it.

Change the look and
style of text on your
slides.

Add photographs or
other images.

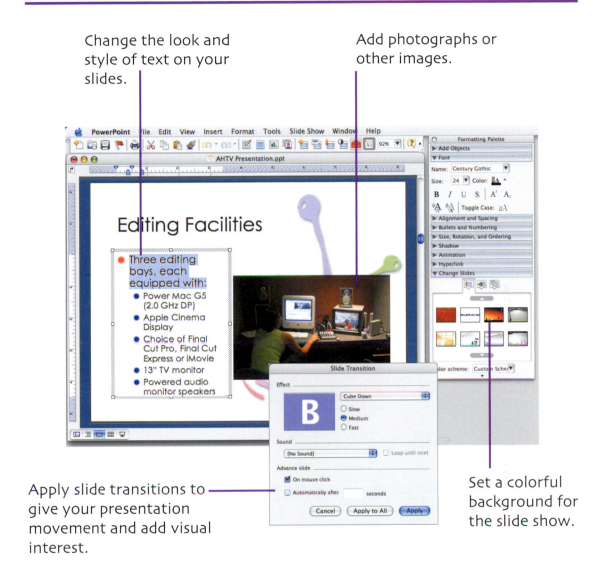

Apply slide transitions to
give your presentation
movement and add visual
interest.

Set a colorful
background for
the slide show.

how this book works

The title of each section explains what is covered on that page.

Important terms and Web site addresses are shown in orange.

Numbered steps explain actions to perform in a specific order.

Captions explain what you're doing and why. They also point to items of interest.

set slide effects (Mac)

Like its Windows sibling, PowerPoint for Mac gives you two ways to control slide effects. Preset animations apply simple animations to the elements on the slide; custom animation gives you more control over each element (though not, alas, as much control as PowerPoint for Windows).

To use a preset animation, first choose View > Normal, then display the slide to which you want to apply the preset. Next, choose Slide Show > Preset Animations, then choose a preset from the cascading menu. The animation is applied to the slide.

Custom animations are a bit more complex to apply, but are much more flexible.

1 Begin by choosing View > Normal, then display the slide to which you want to apply the animation.

2 Choose Slide Show > Custom Animation. The Custom Animation dialog appears.

Preview pane

make it move

The extra bits section at the end of each chapter contains additional tips and tricks that you might like to know—but that aren't absolutely necessary for creating the presentation.

The heading for each group of tips matches the section title.

extra bits

rearrange slides p. 82

- If you want to move a group of slides at one time, in Slide Sorter View, click on the first slide, hold down the Shift key, and click the last slide. Those two slides and all slides in between will be selected, and you can drag and drop them as a group.

set slide transitions p. 84

- You can also select multiple slides in the Slide Sorter by clicking in a blank space between slides, then dragging over the slides you want.
- By default, PowerPoint is set so ... ggered ... se dur... But you ... he ... the ... ne to ... ically ... after ... nds. ... little ... hen it ... ions. ... k Pane ... review ... humb... , but ... y button

to trigger the preview manually, and the Slide Show button puts PowerPoint into Slide Show mode, allowing you to see the slides and transitions full screen.

Mac users must apply a transition, then test it in the Slide Show or the small Animation Preview window.

To open the Animation Preview

window, choose Slide Show > Animation Preview. Click anywhere in the window to see the preview play.

- You can purchase add-ins (programs that extend PowerPoint) that give you additional slide transitions beyond the ones that come with PowerPoint. One well-known maker of these add-ins is Crystal Graphics (www.crystalgraphics.com), with their PowerPlugs series.

93

set slide transitions

Transitions between slides can enhance your presentation's message and add visual interest to your show. You can add transitions to one or more slides at one time in either the Normal or Slide Sorter View (though I find it's usually easier to use Slide Sorter View). PowerPoint includes dozens of special transition effects to choose from, ranging from subtle to the polar opposite of subtle. With slide transitions, as with any animation in PowerPoint, you should live by the principle "less is more" when choosing transitions, because the flashier they are, the more quickly your audience will become tired of them.

1 Switch to Slide Sorter View to begin setting the transition; choose View > Slide Sorter.

2 Select the slides to which you want to apply the transitions. To select multiple slides, click on the first slide, hold down the Shift key, and click the last slide. Those slides and all slides in between are selected.

3 Choose Slide Show > Slide Transition.

On Windows, the Slide Transition Task Pane opens.

Transition list

Transition speed

Sound pop-up menu

84   make it move

The page number next to the heading makes it easy to refer back to the main content.

useful tools

PowerPoint comes with most of what you need to create a terrific presentation, but you can improve the presentation with an image editor, which allows you to touch up and resize photos, modify images, and create custom backgrounds for your presentation.

Many digital cameras and scanners come bundled with some kind of image editor, such as Adobe Photoshop Elements. There are also low-cost or even free image editors, such as Windows Paint or GraphicConverter X for the Mac, as shown.

If you'll be adding links to your slides, you'll want to preview what happens when you click on those links in a Web browser. On Windows, you'll probably use Internet Explorer, and on the Mac, Safari (shown).

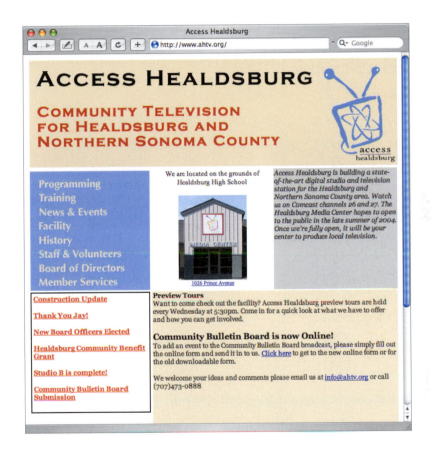

the next step

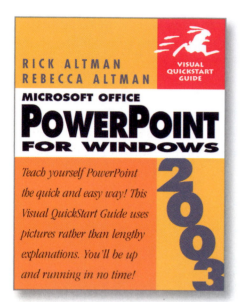

While this Visual QuickProject Guide will walk you through all of the steps required to create a presentation and deliver it to an audience, there's more to learn about PowerPoint. After you complete your QuickProject, consider picking up one of two books, also published by Peachpit Press, as an in-depth, handy reference.

If you're using PowerPoint for Windows, check out Microsoft Office PowerPoint 2003 for Windows: Visual QuickStart Guide, by Rick and Rebecca Altman.

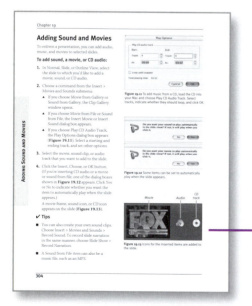

If you're using PowerPoint for Macintosh, take a look at Microsoft Office 2004 for Mac OS X: Visual QuickStart Guide, by Steve Schwartz.

Both books give you clear examples, concise, step-by-step instructions, and many helpful tips that will help you improve your presentations.

1. explore powerpoint

Before you get started on your presentation, you need to see the tools that PowerPoint gives you. In this chapter, you'll explore the user interface from two versions of PowerPoint: PowerPoint 2003 for Windows and PowerPoint 2004 for Macintosh. You'll see that they aren't terribly different.

Start up PowerPoint. On Windows, point at the Start menu, choose Programs, then choose Microsoft Office, then choose Microsoft Office PowerPoint 2003.

On the Mac, open the Applications folder, then open the Microsoft Office 2004 folder, and double-click on the Microsoft PowerPoint icon.

When PowerPoint starts, it creates a new presentation document. In this chapter, you'll create your presentation file, set it up for subsequent chapters, and save the file. You'll add text and graphics to this new document as you build the presentation throughout the rest of the book.

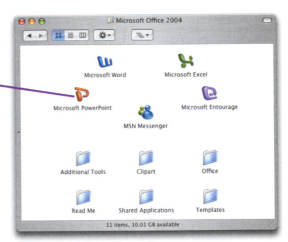

2003 for windows

PowerPoint 2003 for Windows has a main document window where you'll write your presentation and dress up your slides. In this picture, the Power-Point window is in the Normal view.

A The Menu Bar

B The Standard Toolbar has buttons and pop-up menus with the most-used commands, such as Save, Print, and Undo.

C The Formatting Toolbar allows you to style text on your slides, as well as change the slide design and create a new slide.

D The Normal View Pane has two tabs. The Slides tab that is shown here displays thumbnails of the presentation's slides, including the slide's graphics. The Outline tab shows you just the text on each slide; you'll learn more about how to use this tab in Chapter 2.

E The Slide Pane shows you what the current slide looks like. In this case, the slide is showing placeholders for text that you'll put on the slide later.

F This is the Task Pane, which changes its contents depending on what you are doing. You don't need to use it at this point in the project, so close it by clicking the X in its upper-right corner, or by pressing Control-F1.

G The Notes Pane is where you can type speaker notes for each slide. These notes will appear on printed handouts, but not in the onscreen presentation.

H The View Buttons let you switch between three different ways to look at your presentation.

I The Drawing Toolbar allows you to draw shapes on your slides, such as circles, lines, and arrows.

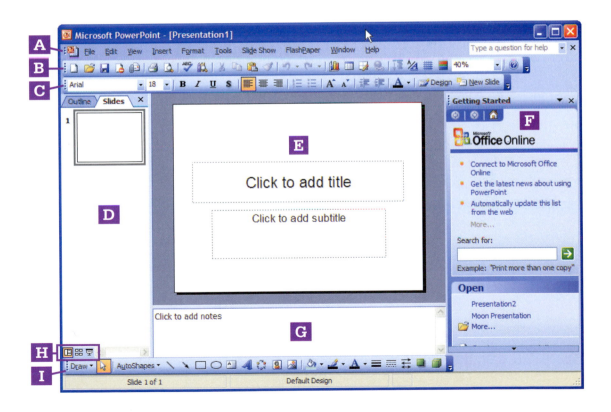

2004 for macintosh

Like its Windows counterpart, PowerPoint 2004 for Macintosh has a main document window, where you have the slide, the outline, and the space for speaker notes.

A The Standard Toolbar has buttons and pop-up menus with the most-used commands, such as Save, Print, and Undo.

In the Normal View shown here, the PowerPoint window is split into three panes.

B The Outline Pane is where you'll type the text of your presentation.

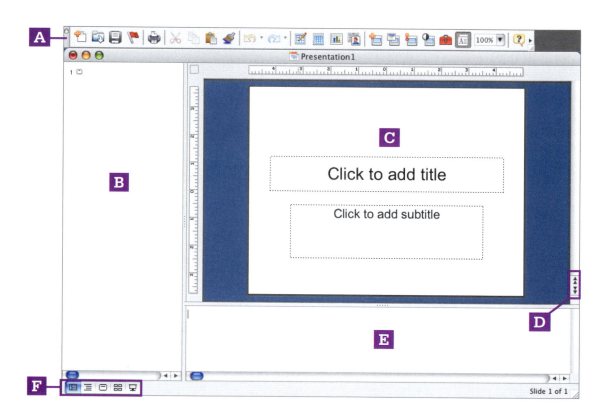

C The Slide Pane shows you what the current slide looks like. The slide is surrounded by the horizontal and vertical rulers, which can help you position graphics and text on the slide. You don't need to use the rulers at this point in the project, so choose View > Ruler to hide them.

D The Previous Slide and Next Slide buttons let you step through the slides in the presentation.

E The Notes Pane is where you can type speaker notes for each slide. These notes will appear on printed handouts, but not in the onscreen presentation.

F The View Buttons let you switch between five different ways to look at your presentation.

The Formatting Palette contains most of the commands and buttons you need to modify the look of your slides and the text and graphics on the slides. It changes to match what you're doing, and has different sections that appear and disappear as needed. See Chapter 5 for more about using the Formatting Palette.

explore toolbars

In PowerPoint you'll use many toolbars to change the look of your slides and the things that you put on the slides. For now, we'll look at the buttons in the Standard Toolbar that you will use the most in your project.

Use the New button to create a new presentation.

The Open button lets you open existing presentation files.

Click the Save button at any time to save your work.

Use the Cut, Copy, and Paste buttons to move text or graphics from one place to another in your presentation, or even to other presentations (or other programs).

The Undo and Redo buttons help you recover from mistakes.

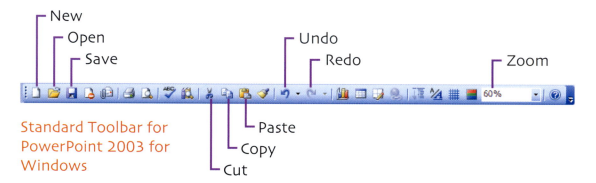

Standard Toolbar for PowerPoint 2003 for Windows

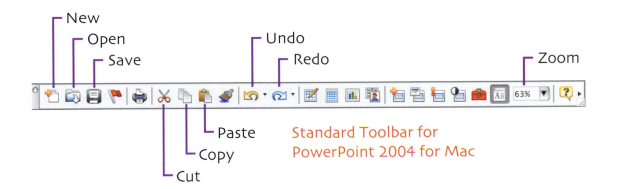

New
Open
Save
Undo
Redo
Zoom

Paste
Copy
Cut

Standard Toolbar for
PowerPoint 2004 for Mac

Use the Zoom menu to make the slide in the Slide Pane larger or smaller.

400%
300%
200%
150%
✓ 100%
75%
66%
50%
33%
25%
Fit

Use the Fit choice in this menu to make the slide fill the pane.

explore powerpoint

powerpoint views

PowerPoint 2003 for Windows has three view buttons.

You saw the Normal View earlier in this chapter.

The Slide Sorter View allows you to rearrange slides by dragging and dropping them into a different order. Each slide is shown as a thumbnail, along with the slide's number. You'll learn more about this view in Chapter 7.

The Slide Show View starts the slide show, allowing you to preview your presentation full-screen. This is also the view you use to actually give the presentation.

PowerPoint 2004 for Mac uses five view buttons.

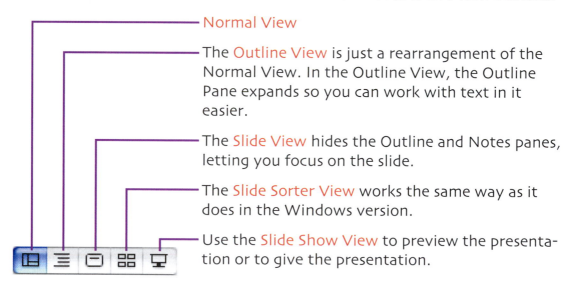

Normal View

The Outline View is just a rearrangement of the Normal View. In the Outline View, the Outline Pane expands so you can work with text in it easier.

The Slide View hides the Outline and Notes panes, letting you focus on the slide.

The Slide Sorter View works the same way as it does in the Windows version.

Use the Slide Show View to preview the presentation or to give the presentation.

explore powerpoint

anatomy of a slide

To make it easier to create your slides, PowerPoint provides placeholders on its slides into which you can put text, graphics, or charts. These placeholders are arranged into preset slide layouts, and every slide in your presentation is based on one of these layouts. Besides the slide layout, each presentation also has a single design template, which provides the visual look of the slide, including things like the background image for the slides and the style and color of the text you put on the slides.

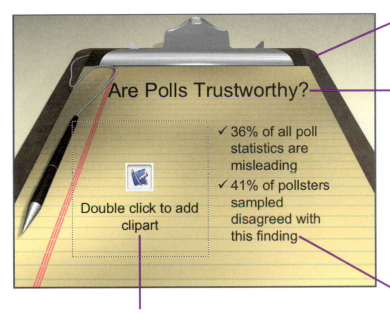

The Background is an image that is part of the design template.

A Title is included on each slide layout (except for the Blank layout). The title corresponds to the main heading for each slide in the presentation's outline. You'll learn more about outlines in Chapter 2.

A slide's Body Text is contained in one or more text boxes. The body text can be bulleted or numbered lists, a caption for an image, or plain text.

Slide layouts with slots for graphics, charts, or movies come with Placeholders that tell you where to add the object.

save the presentation

Save your presentation file before you continue to the next chapter. Choose File > Save.

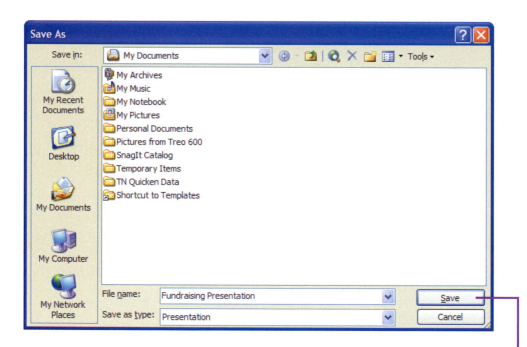

The first time you save, the Save As box appears. This is where you name the presentation. Type the name you want in the File name box (on the Mac, in the Save As box), then click the Save button.

extra bits

2004 for macintosh p. 4

- Don't be thrown by the Drawing Toolbar that's in the figure for PowerPoint for Windows. The Mac version has a Drawing Toolbar, too; it's just not shown at the moment.

anatomy of a slide p. 9

- Not shown on page 4 are a slide's header or footer. You can have one or both of these on each slide. Headers (at the top of each slide) and footers (at the bottom) can contain slide numbers, the date and time, a copyright notice, or any other information you want to include.

save the presentation p. 10

- Save all of the files used in the project in a single folder you create inside your My Documents folder (Windows) or Documents folder (Mac). That way, everything you need for the presentation is in one place.

2. write your presentation

Now that you've created your presentation file, you need to write the presentation. And the best place to write the presentation is not on the slides, but in PowerPoint's Outline View. Now, it's possible that, like many of us, you were scared off of outlines by your sixth grade teacher. You should reconsider, because Outline View is PowerPoint's secret weapon for making better presentations. When you write in the outline, you can focus on the content of your presentation, rather than getting distracted by the look of the presentation. Text that you write in the Outline pane will also appear on your slides, and vice versa.

We've all seen PowerPoint presentations where the presenter spent more time on the appearance than the message. But your message is the most important part of your presentation. PowerPoint's biggest trap is seducing you with flashy pictures, distracting you from your message. By writing the presentation in the outline before you even consider the look, you'll avoid that pitfall—and you'll be way ahead of most other presenters.

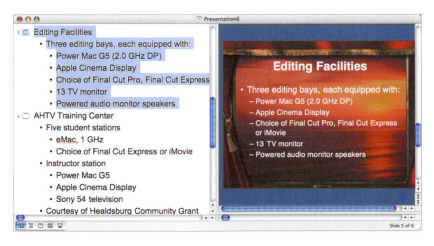

You don't need to do anything extra to get an outline; every presentation has an outline underneath, so it makes sense to start in the outline, rather than on the slide.

write the outline

Switch to Outline View by clicking the Outline tab in the Normal View pane (Windows) or by clicking the Outline View button at the bottom of the PowerPoint window (Mac).

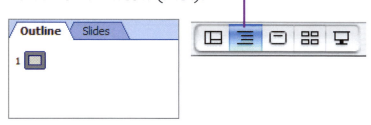

When Outline View becomes active, the Outline pane becomes bigger, to make room for you to work, but you can still see a preview of the slide in the Slide pane. If you need even more room in the outline, point at the border between the Outline pane and the Slide pane; when the cursor becomes a double-headed arrow, drag the border so the pane is as wide as you want.

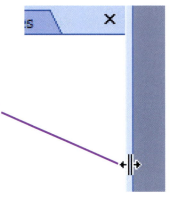

The first slide is a Title slide, which contains the title and subtitle for the presentation. The first line, or heading, in your outline is the title of your presentation. Type it, then press Enter (Return).

Hey, what's this? PowerPoint created a new slide, rather than letting you type the subtitle on the first slide.

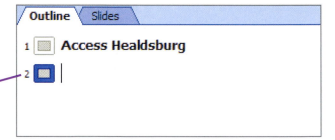

No problem; press the Tab key. That tells PowerPoint that you want to create a subheading, which is a heading indented below an existing heading.

You can see from the slide preview that your slide is looking the way that you want.

You're done for now with the Title slide (we'll dress it up with graphics in later chapters), so choose Insert > New Slide. PowerPoint creates the new slide, and automatically assigns it the Title and Text layout (which is called Bulleted List on Mac).

Type the title of the second slide, press Enter (Return), then press Tab and type the bullet points for your second slide, pressing Return between each bullet point. As you type, the slide preview updates. When you're done with the slide, press Enter (Return), then press Shift-Tab to get a new slide. Continue for the rest of your presentation.

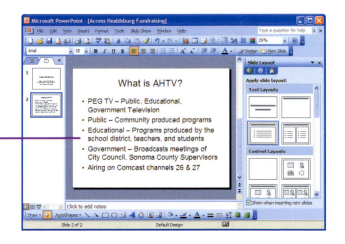

work with outline text

The flexibility of PowerPoint's Outline View is that it makes it easy to rearrange your ideas as you work on your presentation. Let's look at the outline for the last slide we wrote:

> 2 **What is AHTV?**
> • PEG TV – Public, Educational, Government Television
> • Public – Community produced programs
> • Educational – Programs produced by the school district, teachers, and students
> • Government – Broadcasts meetings of City Council, Sonoma County Supervisors
> • Airing on Comcast channels 26 & 27

It's okay, but it needs better organization. Some headings can move up and others would be better as subheadings. To move headings around, use the Outlining toolbar. Display it by choosing View > Toolbars > Outlining.

Click Promote to move a heading left, making it a higher outline level.

Click Demote to move a heading right.

The Move Up and Move Down buttons move a heading and any subheads up or down in the outline.

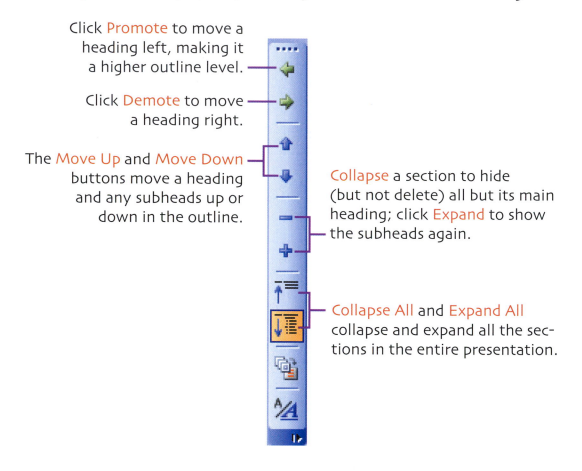

Collapse a section to hide (but not delete) all but its main heading; click Expand to show the subheads again.

Collapse All and Expand All collapse and expand all the sections in the entire presentation.

Click anywhere in a heading, then use a button in the Outlining toolbar to move it. After a few strategic moves, the outline is better organized.

Outline

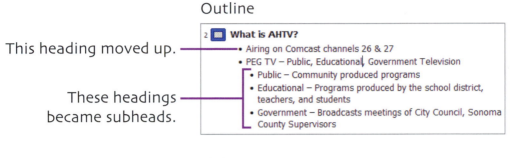

This heading moved up.

These headings became subheads.

Slide

write outline in Word

If you prefer to do your writing in Word, that's no problem; you can create an outline in Word, save it, then import the outline into PowerPoint.

In Word, Choose View > Outline. Word's Outlining toolbar (which resembles the one in PowerPoint) appears automatically.

You can write the outline and move headings around in much the same way that you can in PowerPoint.

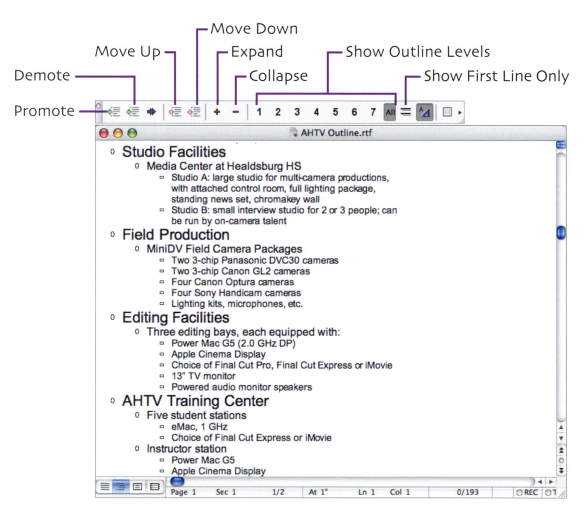

When you're done in Word, you must save the document in a format that PowerPoint can read, called Rich Text Format (RTF). Choose File > Save As, then from the Save as type pop-up menu (the Format pop-up menu on Mac), choose Rich Text Format, then click Save.

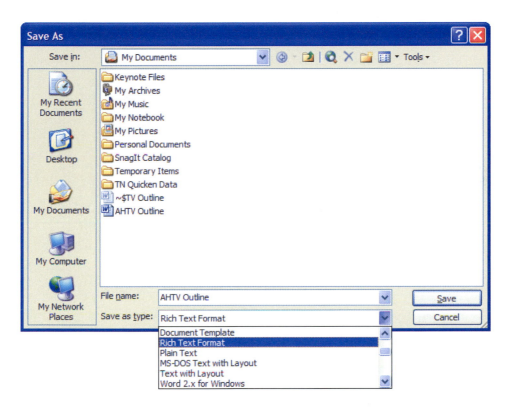

Back in PowerPoint, choose File > Open, select the RTF file, and click Open. PowerPoint converts the file into a presentation.

use the research pane

When you're writing a presentation, you often need to look up a bit of information here, check a fact there, or use a thesaurus to find a better word. The Research pane, found in PowerPoint 2003 for Windows, gives you instant access to reference materials, both online and on your machine.PowerPoint for Macintosh does not include this feature.

Open the Research pane by choosing View > Task Pane (Ctrl-F1), and then choose Research from the pop-up menu at the top of the Task Pane.

If you want to look up a word, the easiest way to do it is to hold down the Alt key and click the word. It will appear in the Search for field of the Research pane, with the Encarta Dictionary definition.

You can also type a word or phrase in the Search for field and press Enter to start a search.

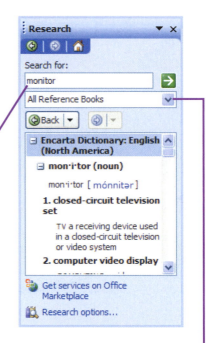

If you want to use a different reference source (say, you would rather do a thesaurus lookup, or search the online Encarta Encyclopedia), choose the source from the Source pop-up menu (the one directly under the search field).

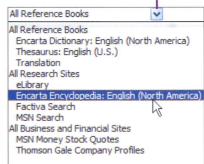

write your presentation

extra bits

write your presentation p. 13

- Having problems getting started writing the presentation? PowerPoint's AutoContent Wizard provides you with the basic outline for many types of presentations, such as Selling a Product or Service, Marketing Plan, Company Meeting, Recommending a Strategy, and many more. These outlines are a good starting point when you're in a hurry, or when you're just not feeling inspired. To use the AutoContent Wizard in PowerPoint for Windows, choose File > New (or press Ctrl-N), then in the Task Pane, click From AutoContent Wizard. The Wizard will start up. In PowerPoint for Macintosh, choose File > Project Gallery, or press Cmd-Shift-P. In the Blank Documents group, double-click AutoContent Wizard.

write the outline p. 14

- If the text in the outline is too small to work with comfortably, choose a larger value from the Zoom menu in the Standard toolbar. Don't change the font size in the Formatting Toolbar (Windows) or Formatting palette (Mac); that changes the size of text on the slides, but doesn't affect the outline text.

work with outline text p. 16

- If you prefer, you can move headings around with the mouse. When you place the pointer over the icon of a slide or a bullet in the outline, the pointer changes to a four-headed arrow. Click and drag the heading to a new location. You can move headings this way in either PowerPoint or Word.

extra bits

write outline in Word p. 18

- If you're dealing with a large presentation, you have a large outline. And Word, being a full-fledged word processor, has better tools for working with larger outlines. For example, you have more control over the number of heading levels that you show or hide at any given time, which lets you concentrate on the points that are important without being distracted by supporting information.

use the research pane p. 20

- To look up words another way, right-click a word in your presentation, then choose Look Up from the shortcut menu. The word will be transferred to the Research pane and will be looked up in the reference source you last used.

- The Research pane has a Translation reference source. You can use it to translate a word or short phrase to and from a very wide variety of languages.

write your presentation

3. gather image and sound files

Now that you've written your presentation outline, I'll let you in on a secret: The hardest part of creating your presentation is behind you. From this point, you're adding more elements to the presentation to add impact to the story you're telling and making the slides look good. But before we plunge into the nitty-gritty of changing the look of your slides, there's still one more important bit of planning to do. You need to decide what parts of your presentation will be enhanced with the addition of pictures and media files such as sounds and video. We've all seen PowerPoint presentations where the speaker threw in pictures and sounds seemingly at random, and that tends to turn audiences off. A quick review of your slides helps you avoid this pitfall.

In this chapter, we'll figure out where images, sounds, and even video clips could enhance your presentation, find images, and talk a bit about using sound in PowerPoint slideshows.

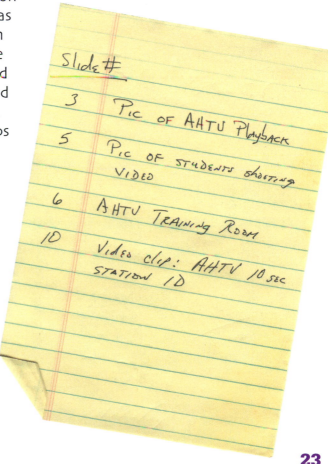

Slide #

3   Pic of AHTV Playback

5   Pic of students shooting video

6   AHTV Training Room

10   Video clip: AHTV 10 sec station ID

review your slides

For the first time, we're going to look at material on the slides, rather than in the outline, with an eye to deciding where we want to add images or sounds. You'll need a notepad or scratch paper to take notes as you browse the slides.

On Windows, click the Slides tab, and if needed, drag the border between the Normal View pane and the Slide pane to make the slide thumbnails easier to read.

Click the Normal View button at the bottom of the PowerPoint window, or choose View > Normal.

On Mac, you'll use the Normal View as is, working with the Outline and Slide panes.

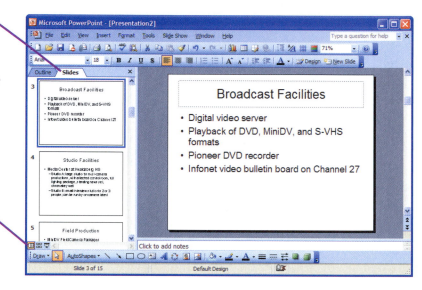

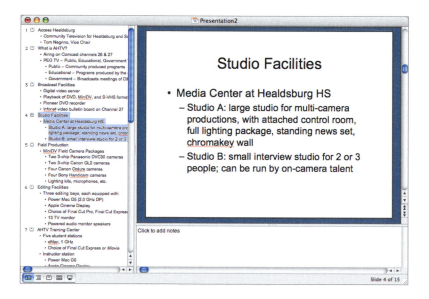

gather image and sound files

If you want more room for the slide, point at the border between the Slides and Notes panes and drag it down to hide the Notes pane.

Using the Previous Slide and Next Slide buttons, browse through your slides, and as you re-read the contents of each slide, think about what pictures you could add to the slide that would help your audience better grasp your message. Some slides won't need any help from images; others will benefit from an added image. For example, on the slide in my presentation about the Training Facility, a picture of the facility would be helpful, because it's a good-looking facility.

As you browse, jot down notes with the slide number and what sorts of images, sound files, or even video clips you could add that would enhance the slide.

view slide layouts

Now that you know what sorts of images you might want to use, it's time to start thinking about how those images will appear on your slides. You'll do this by looking at the slide layouts PowerPoint provides for slides that contain images, or images and text.

On Windows, display the Task Pane by choosing View > Task Pane, or press Ctrl-F1. From the pop-up menu at the top of the Task Pane, choose Slide Layout. The Slide Layouts appear.

Scroll down to Content Layouts, which have placeholders for one or more pictures, or a title and pictures.

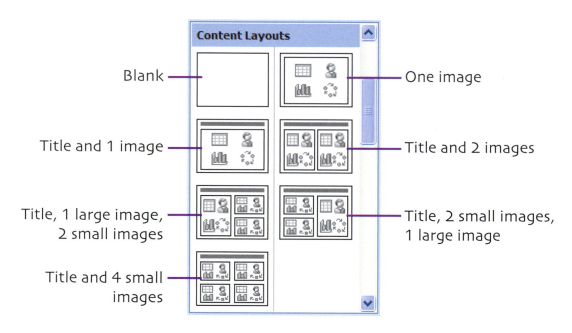

Blank

One image

Title and 1 image

Title and 2 images

Title, 1 large image, 2 small images

Title, 2 small images, 1 large image

Title and 4 small images

gather image and sound files

For your slides, you might find the Text and Content Layouts more useful; these include placeholders for a title, bulleted text, and one or more pictures.

Title, text, and 1 image

Title, 1 image, and text

Title, text, and 2 small images

Title, 2 small images, and text

Title and text over 1 image

Title and 1 image over text

Title and 2 small images over text

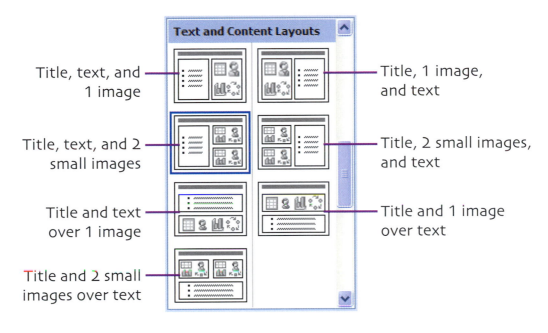

Mac PowerPoint users will find slide layouts in the Change Slides section of the Formatting Palette. If the Formatting Palette isn't visible, choose View > Formatting Palette.

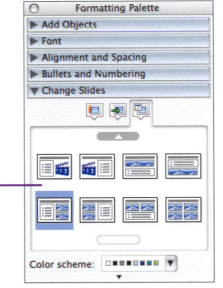

gather image and sound files

As you browse through the slide layouts, you can see how a slide will look with that layout applied by displaying the slide, then clicking on the thumbnail of a layout. The slide will change to the new layout, reformatting the slide's text if necessary.

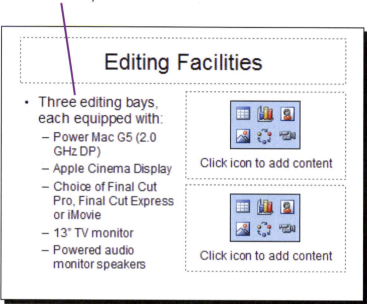

find images

Images you use in your presentations can come from many possible sources: digital pictures you take yourself; scanned photographs or drawings; stock photography that you purchase online; or clip art. Some clip art comes with Microsoft Office. You can find it by choosing Insert > Picture > Clip Art. The Clip Art pane of the Task Pane opens (Windows). On the Mac, it opens the Clip Gallery.

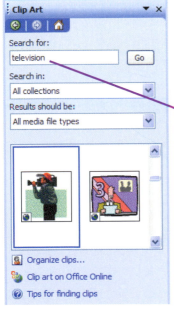

On Windows, search the clip art by entering a word in the Search for field, then click Go. On the Mac, enter a word in the Search field, then click Search.

find images (cont.)

You'll add images to your slides in Chapter 6. For now, look through the available images in the clip art collections to find images that you may want to use.

If you're not happy with the selection of clip art that comes with the program, there's a lot more available for free at Microsoft Office Online, at http://office.Microsoft.com/clipart/.

If you find any images that you like among the vast collection on Microsoft Office Online, download them to your local machine for later use.

choose sounds

Finding sounds is a bit trickier than finding images. The Windows version of PowerPoint includes sound files in its clip art collection, but the Mac version does not.

To find sounds on Windows, restrict your search to just sounds in the Results should be pop-up menu in the Clip Art pane.

Uncheck the Clip Art, Photographs, and Movies choices.

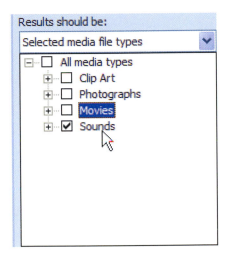

Search the collection by entering a word in the Search for field, then click Go. The sounds will appear in the results field as icons.

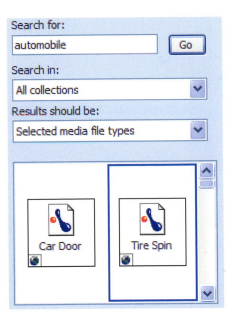

choose sounds (cont.)

Once you find sounds, you'll want to hear them. Right-click on a sound, and from the shortcut menu, choose Preview/Properties. The Preview/Properties dialog appears and plays your sound.

Play button —

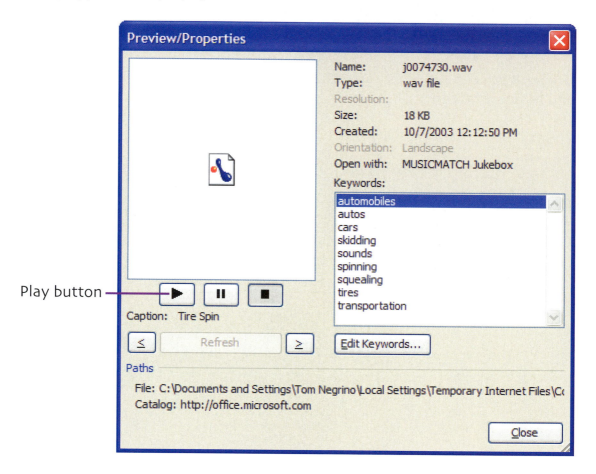

If you need to play the sound again, click the Play button.

You'll add sounds to slides in Chapter 6. For now, make note of the sounds that would work with your presentation.

extra bits

view slide layouts p. 26

- Windows users have 27 preset slide layouts; Mac users have 24.

find images p. 29

- Images you use in your presentations should be royalty free, meaning they can be used without additional payments to the image's producer.

- Clip art and other media found at the Microsoft Office Online site are subject to certain restrictions, which are listed at the site. At the bottom of the clip art page, you'll find a link called "Legal." Click it, and be prepared to be stunned into submission by legal-eze.

- There are many places online to find images for your presentations. Rather than singling out just a few companies, do a Google search on all of the following search terms: "images" "royalty-free" "clip art". You'll get a wealth of choices, some free, some not.

- Besides online resources, you can find many excellent clip art packages on the market. These come on CD or DVD, and are usually royalty free. Some good ones are from Hemera (www.hemera.com), in their Photo-Object collections, and Nova Development's Art Explosion (www.novadevelopment.com). Digital Juice (www.digitaljuice.com) has the Presenters Toolkit package, which contains thousands of images, video clips, animations, and backgrounds.

choose sounds p. 31

- You can find many Web sites that sell royalty-free sound collections, such as SoundRangers (www.soundrangers.com). These sites sell individual sounds for as little as $1.50. You'll find more sites with a Google search on "sounds" "royalty-free". Most of these sites work equally well for both Windows and Mac users.

- Just because Mac Office's Clip Gallery doesn't come with sounds, it doesn't mean that you can't either add sounds to the Clip Gallery, or use sounds from any sound file in your presentations.

4. pick a design

With your presentation's content set, it's time to start dressing up your slides. You'll do that in this chapter by selecting a design template for your presentation. That template provides the visual look of the slides—the slide design—throughout the whole presentation, including elements like a background image for the slides and the style and color of the text you put on the slides.

You'll also apply a slide layout to each slide in your presentation, matching the layout to the content of the slide. For example, you'll apply the Title layout to the first slide, and add one of the layouts that contains image placeholders for slides where you will add pictures.

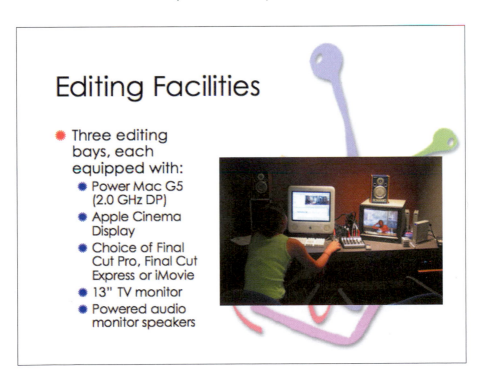

pick a slide design

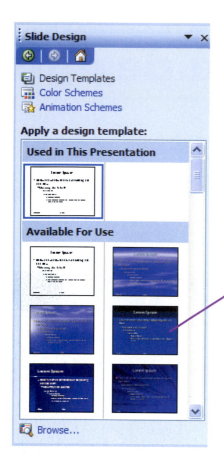

When you pick a slide design, PowerPoint applies it to all of the slides in the presentation, so that they will have a consistent look. Begin adding a slide design by displaying one of the presentation's slides in Normal View. Any slide will do, but I usually use one of the slides that contains a title and bulleted text, because those are the most common in presentations.

On Windows, display the Task Pane by choosing View > Task Pane, or press Ctrl-F1. From the pop-up menu at the top of the Task Pane, choose Slide Design. The slide designs appear as small thumbnail images.

On the Mac, you'll find the slide templates in the Change Slides section of the Formatting Palette.

Click the Slide Design tab.

pick a design

Scroll through the slide designs until you find one that you like. Click the thumbnail of the slide design, and PowerPoint applies it to your slide.

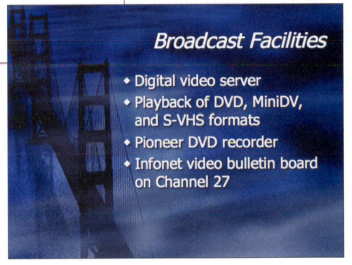

You can see how applying the slide design has changed the font and styles of the text on the slide; the positioning of the text on the slide; the slide's background image; and the style of the bullets used on the slide (from dots to diamonds).

apply slide layouts

Now it's time to go through all of your slides and apply the proper slide layout to each one.

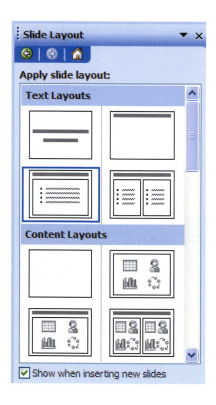

On Windows, from the pop-up menu at the top of the Task Pane, choose Slide Layout.

Scroll to the first slide in your presentation, which is the title slide. The slide should be using the Title Slide or Title Only layout. If it is not (it usually isn't if you imported the slide outline from Word, for example), click the layout you want.

On the Mac, click the Slide Layout tab in the Change Slides section of the Formatting Palette.

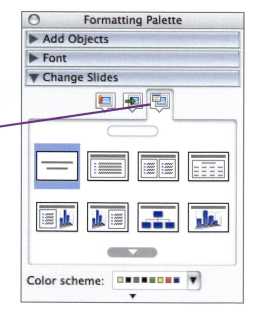

pick a design

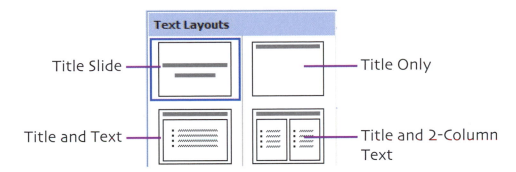

Title Slide — Title Only
Title and Text — Title and 2-Column Text

The slide changes to the new layout.

Slide with Title and Text layout

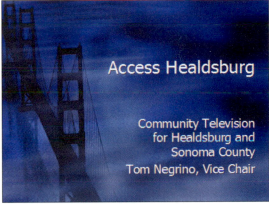

Slide with Title Slide layout

Use the Next Slide button (at the right edge of the PowerPoint window) to move through your slides, applying the appropriate layout to each one. This is where the notes you took in Chapter 3 will come in handy; because you've already figured out where images will go in your presentation, you can apply picture layouts where it is appropriate. If you're doing a presentation that includes charts, apply one of the layouts that has chart placeholders.

customize background

Let's say you like the font and bullet styles of a slide design, but not the background image—you can choose the slide design, then change just the background to one more appropriate for your presentation. Of course if you're happy with the background, you can skip this step.

For my presentation for Access Healdsburg, I found a slide design that was pretty good, but it had a wildly inappropriate background image for a community television station.

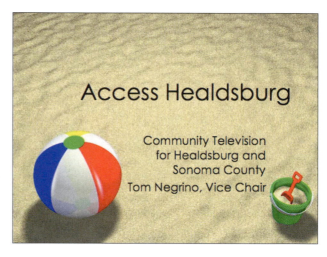

So I replaced that image with an image of the organization's logo that I prepared in Adobe Photoshop.

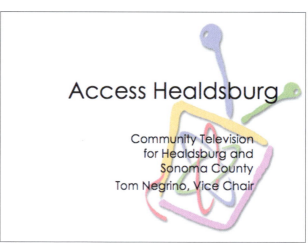

To use your own background image, choose Format > Background (Format > Slide Background), which brings up the Background dialog.

From the pop-up menu at the bottom of the dialog, choose Fill Effects. In the resulting Fill Effects dialog, click the Picture tab, then click the Select Picture button.

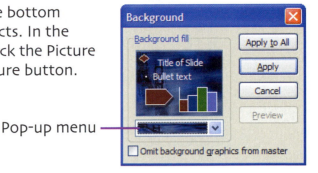

Pop-up menu ——

The Select Picture dialog will appear. Find the image file you want to use as the background and click Insert. You'll return to the Fill Effects dialog, which displays a preview of the picture you just chose.

Click OK to return to the Background dialog. You want the new background to appear on all your slides, so click Apply to All.

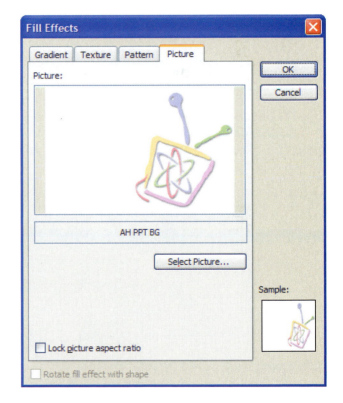

adjust text location

After applying the slide design and possibly customizing the background, you may find that some of the text on your slides isn't quite where you want it. For example, the title slide of my presentation had the two placeholders containing the title and subtitle covering the organization's logo.

The text on the slide is in placeholders, and you can move the placeholders as you like.

Text placeholders

Move the pointer towards the text on a slide. As you get near the text, the pointer will change to a four-headed arrow (on the Mac it will change to a grabber hand).

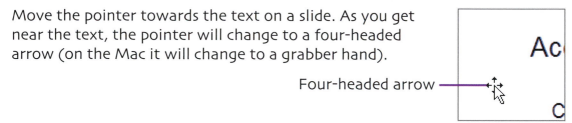

Four-headed arrow

Selection handles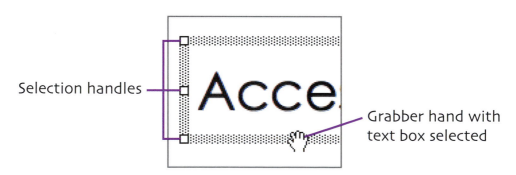

Grabber hand with text box selected

When the pointer changes, click the mouse button. The text placeholder will be selected, showing a thick dotted border. You can drag the placeholder from any spot on the border. Clicking and dragging any of the placeholder's selection handles resizes the placeholder.

After the placeholders are moved around, the logo is mostly uncovered, and the slide looks much better.

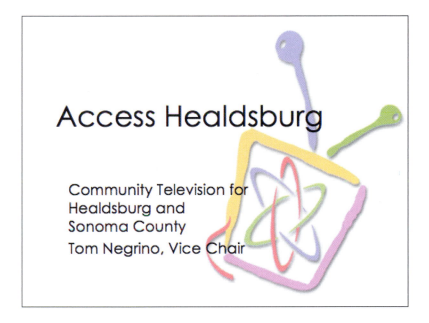

extra bits

pick a slide design p. 36

- The little thumbnails of the design templates in the Task Pane (Windows) or Formatting Palette (Mac) might not be large enough for you to get a good feel for the template. To get a bigger view, click the Browse link at the bottom of the Task Pane, or on the Mac, choose Format > Slide Design. You'll get a dialog box that shows you a larger preview of the template.

- The Windows and Mac versions of PowerPoint don't come with the same set of design templates. Windows PowerPoint comes with 63 different templates, and the Mac version checks in with 110 templates. All templates are compatible across platforms, and are part of the presentation file, so if you start working on a presentation on a Mac, then copy it to Windows, the slide template will come right along.

pick a design

apply slide layouts p. 38

- To apply a slide template that is different from the main template that you're using to more than one slide, switch to Slide Sorter View, and select the slides you want to change. You can Shift-click slide thumbnails to select multiple consecutive slides, or Ctrl-click (Cmd-click) multiple nonconsecutive slides.

- Not happy with the slide templates that come with PowerPoint? There are many places to find more templates on the Web. The first place to look is Microsoft Office Online, at http://office.microsoft.com/templates/. Click the PowerPoint link to display additional design templates, background slides, and useful templates for things like calendars, charts and diagrams, and awards and certificates. All of these templates are free, and work on both Windows or Mac.

- There are many online sites that sell additional templates. Search for "PowerPoint templates" using Google or another search engine.

customize background p. 40

- PowerPoint can use just about any graphic file (in a standard format such as JPEG, TIFF, or PNG) as a slide background. To make a new background, you'll need a graphic editing program, such as Adobe Photoshop or Macromedia Fireworks. Those programs are terrific, but they're not cheap, and you can get by with less expensive alternatives. Windows Paint, which comes with Windows, can do the job of creating a background, and on the Mac, the shareware GraphicConverter (www.lemkesoft.com) is a good choice.

- Just as there are sites that sell slide templates, others sell slide backgrounds. One of my favorites is PowerPoint Art (www.powerpointart.com), which sells a subscription that allows you to use any of their thousands of backgrounds. Again, a Google search will turn up many others.

extra bits

adjust text location p. 42

- You can often make your slides look even better by changing the font size or text alignment. You'll see how to do that in Chapter 5.

5. work with text

Even though you did most of the writing of your presentation in the outline, now that you see the text on the slides with your preferred slide design, you probably want to make some changes on the slides themselves.

In this chapter, you'll learn how to edit and format text on the slides, add hyperlinks, and even add extra text to a slide for special purposes like adding captions to images. Finally, you'll learn how to avoid a major presentation embarrassment: misspellings on your slides.

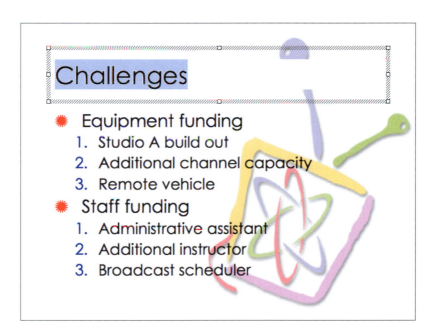

edit slide text

If you want to add text to a slide, move the mouse pointer over the text. The cursor will change into an I-beam, indicating that clicking will set the insertion point where you can start typing.

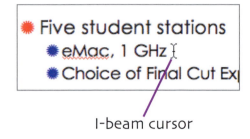

Click the mouse button, and add or delete text.

I-beam cursor

You can also use the I-beam cursor to select text inside a text placeholder. Click and drag over the text you want to select. Once it is selected, you can type to replace the selected text.

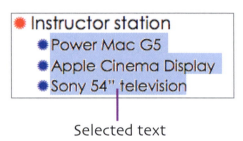

Selected text

The most common reason to want to edit text on a slide is to make the text work better with your slide design, which usually means getting a line of text to break in a different spot. A line break is the point on a line at which the text wraps down to the next line.

For example, let's look again at the title slide of my presentation. For this first slide, it would look better if none of the text in the subhead or my name covered up any of the organization's logo.

To change the text so that it wraps more attractively, we'll add manual line breaks to the text. Click to set the insertion point before the word where you want the break to happen.

You can't just press Enter (Return), because PowerPoint will think that you want to create a new paragraph, which on slides with bulleted text would result in a new bullet point. Instead, press Shift-Enter (Shift-Return), which adds a line break without adding a paragraph break. On the next line, I deleted the comma after my name and added a manual line break. The result is considerably more pleasing to the eye.

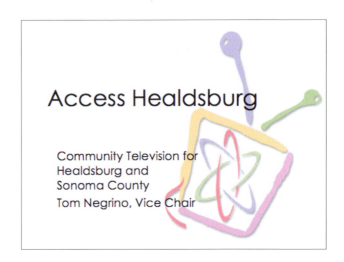

Insertion point

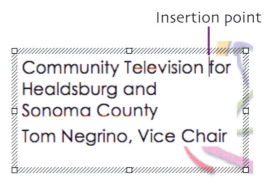

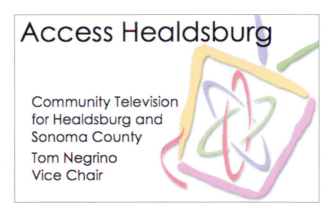

format slide text

Another way to change the text on your slides is to change its formatting, including the size and look of the text, the alignment, and the spacing between the lines.

Most text changes are done in much the same way that you would do them in a word processor: Select the text, then make a choice from the Formatting Toolbar (Windows) or Formatting Palette (Mac).

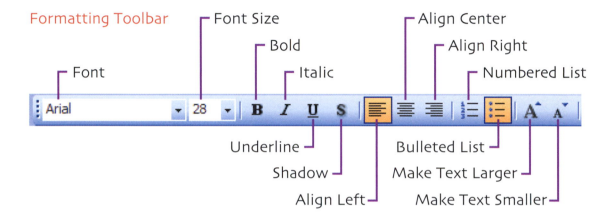

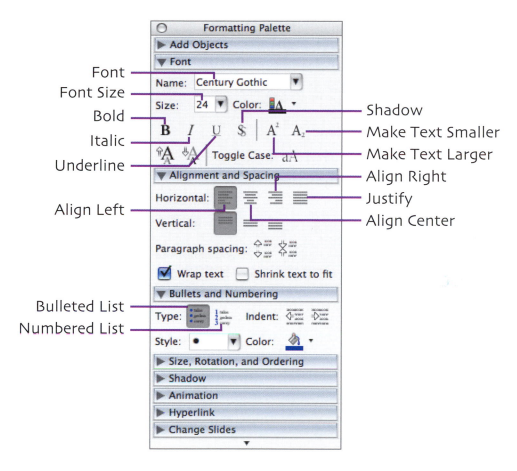

Font — Name: Century Gothic

Font Size — Size: 24

Bold — **B**

Italic — *I*

Underline — U

Shadow — $

Make Text Smaller — A²

Make Text Larger — A₂

Align Right

Justify

Align Left — Horizontal:

Align Center

Bulleted List — Type:

Numbered List

For example, let's say that you want to emphasize some text on one of your slides. First, click and drag to select the text.

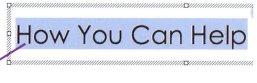

Then click the Italic button on the Formatting Toolbar (Formatting Palette).

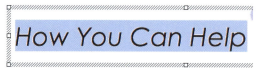

align slide text

When you're working with graphics, you may want to change text alignment in text boxes so that they work better with the image. Or you may decide that left-aligned or right-aligned text looks better on your title slide, instead of the center alignment that is the setting on most design templates.

Production Services

- Full ENG capability
- Multiple-camera productions
- Staff producers and crews ready to shoot your commercial, music video, or industrial

For example, this left-aligned text overlaps the graphic, so the solution is to right-align it.

Select the text, then click one of the text alignment buttons.

Production Services

- Full ENG capability
- Multiple-camera productions
- Staff producers and crews ready to shoot your commercial, music video, or industrial

work with text

change line spacing

You can spread the line spacing on a slide if it is too tight for the content, or reduce the line spacing if you need to get a little more text on the slide.

On this slide, the indented text would be easier to read if the lines were a bit further apart.

What is AHTV?

* Airing on Comcast channels 26 & 27
* PEG TV – Public, Educational, Government Television
  * Public – Community produced programs
  * Educational – Programs produced by the school district, teachers, and students
  * Government – Broadcasts meetings of City Council, Sonoma County Supervisors

Select all of the lines of indented text, then choose Format > Line Spacing. The Line Spacing dialog appears.

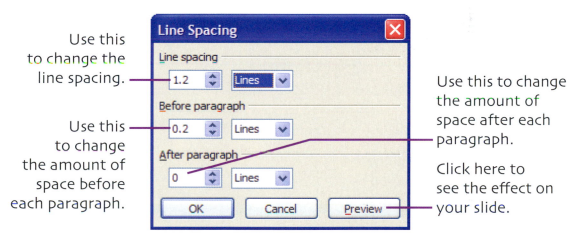

Use this to change the line spacing.

Use this to change the amount of space before each paragraph.

Use this to change the amount of space after each paragraph.

Click here to see the effect on your slide.

Use the spacing controls, then click the Preview button. If you like the new look, click OK. The slide text changes to reflect your new line spacing.

* PEG TV – Public, Educational, Government Television
  * Public – Community produced programs
  * Educational – Programs produced by the school district, teachers, and students
  * Government – Broadcasts meetings of City Council, Sonoma County Supervisors

use numbered lists

Bulleted lists are standard in presentations, but sometimes you want to show a process with a clear beginning and end. For that, a numbered list is better. You can easily change the bulleted list that PowerPoint gives you into a numbered list, and customize the numbering as you wish.

First, select the bulleted text. ——

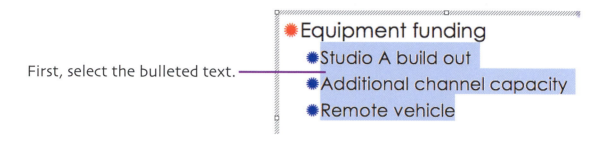

Click the Numbering button in the Formatting Toolbar (Windows) or in the Bullets and Numbering section of the Formatting Palette (Mac).

Numbering button ——

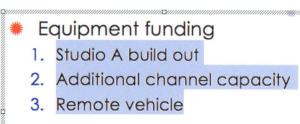

The text changes to a numbered list.

> ❈ Equipment funding
> 1. Studio A build out
> 2. Additional channel capacity
> 3. Remote vehicle

If you want a different numbering system (maybe you would prefer letters rather than numbers, i.e., A, B, C...), with the text still selected, choose Format > Bullets and Numbering. From the resulting dialog, choose a numbering system, then click OK.

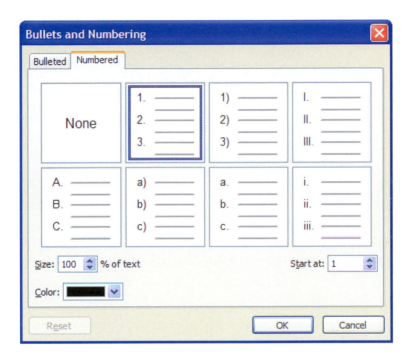

add hyperlinks

You're already familiar with hyperlinks; they're the underlined text that you click on in a Web browser to take you to another Web page. You can use two kinds of hyperlinks in your PowerPoint presentations. The first kind, when clicked during your presentation, leaves PowerPoint, opens the Web browser on your machine, and brings you to the hyperlink's destination. The other kind of hyperlink makes PowerPoint jump to a different slide in your presentation. Either kind of hyperlink only works while you are actually presenting; you don't have to worry about accidentally opening your Web browser while you are working on your presentation.

If you type a Web address into the outline or a PowerPoint slide—such as www.peachpit.com—PowerPoint is smart enough to automatically turn it into a hyperlink. In many instances, that's all you'll need,

✳ Join at our Website
www.ahtv.org

because the link shows your audience the Web address you want them to use and also allows you to click it to display the site.

If you want text on your slide to be the link instead, follow these steps:

1 Select the text that you want to make into a hyperlink.

✳Join at our Website

2 Choose Insert > Hyperlink, or press Ctrl-K (Cmd-K).
The Insert Hyperlink dialog appears.

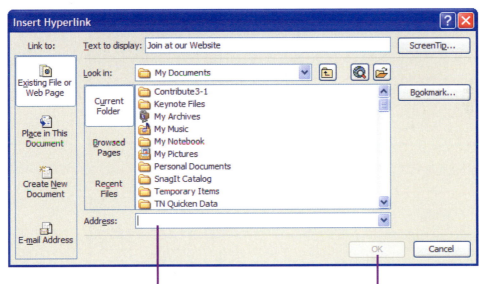

3 In the Address field, type the full Web address for the hyperlink. If the address starts with www., PowerPoint will automatically add the http:// before the address. If it does not, as in office.microsoft.com, you must add the http:// manually.

4 Click OK. The text is colored and underlined, indicating that it has become a hyperlink.

add hyperlinks (cont.)

To make the other kind of hyperlink—the kind that jumps to a different slide in your presentation—follow these steps (this works only in PowerPoint for Windows):

1 Select the text you want to use as the hyperlink and choose Insert > Hyperlink.

2 In the Link section of the Insert Hyperlink dialog, in the Link to section, click Place in This Document. The dialog changes to reflect your choice.

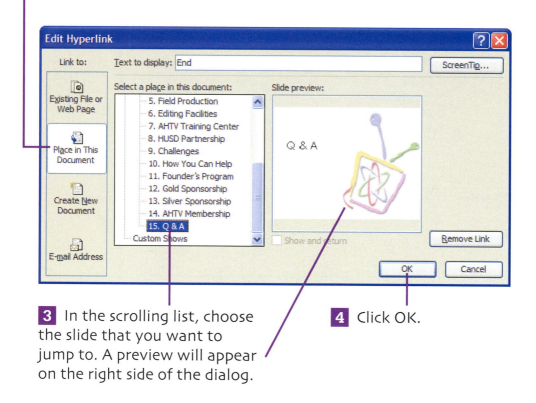

3 In the scrolling list, choose the slide that you want to jump to. A preview will appear on the right side of the dialog.

4 Click OK.

work with text

add text boxes

There are many reasons why you might want text on your slides that isn't part of the outline, but the most common reason to add text is that it will be a label or caption for a picture. To add this text, you'll first need to add a text box to the slide.

 Choose Insert > Text Box.
The cursor changes into the
Insert Text Box cursor.

Click and drag where you want the new text box in order to define its shape of the new text box. When you release the mouse button, the text box appears with a blinking insertion point. Type the text you want in the new text box.

Visit the Media Center at Healdsburg High School!

After you create the text box, you can apply any formatting you like to the text it contains, or adjust the position of the text box on the slide.

check your spelling

Aside from those dreams that you had when you were a kid that you were naked in front of your geometry class (uh, maybe that was just me), there's nothing much more embarrassing than doing a presentation with a misspelled word. Your mistake is there for everyone to see, and it's projected 10 feet wide, to boot! Avoid this nightmare by using PowerPoint's spelling tools.

The nice thing is that PowerPoint is always watching you like a hawk as you write, looking for spelling mistakes. If it finds one, it puts a wavy red underline under the suspected mistake. To fix it, right-click (Control-click) the word. You'll get a shortcut menu with one or more suggested corrections.

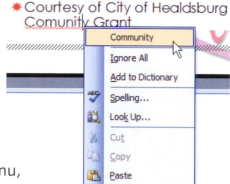

Choose the correction you want from the menu, and PowerPoint replaces the misspelling.

You can also check spelling throughout your whole presentation. Choose Tools > Spelling. The Spelling dialog appears, and finds the first questionable word.

In the Suggestions list, click the correct spelling, then click the Change button. If the word is correct (just not in PowerPoint's dictionary), click Ignore. If you know the word is used more than once in your presentation, you can click the

Change All or Ignore All button, which fixes or ignores all occurrences of the word. When the spelling check is complete, the Spelling dialog closes automatically, and PowerPoint displays an alert box, telling you that it is done.

work with text

extra bits

format slide text p. 50

- When you want to emphasize text, use italic rather than underline. People tend to interpret underlined text as a Web link.

- If you have applied multiple formatting changes to text and you want to make the same changes to other text, you don't have to do all those formatting steps again. Instead, use the Format Painter on the Standard Toolbar, which copies text formatting. First, select the text that has the formatting you want to copy. Then click the Format Painter button.

Click the text you want the formatting copied to, and that text changes to match the first text formatting. If you want to use the Format Painter to apply formatting to more than one text selection, double-click the Format Painter button. This locks the tool on, and whatever text you select will take on the copied formatting. When you're finished applying formatting, click the Format Painter button once to turn it off.

- If you want to change the fonts throughout your presentation, choose Format > Replace Fonts.

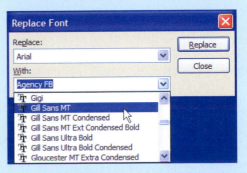

In the resulting dialog, pick the font you want to replace from the Replace pop-up menu, and the new font that you want to use from the With pop-up menu. This is a much faster way to change fonts throughout your presentation, rather than formatting text in individual text boxes.

extra bits

align slide text p. 52

- Sometime it's better to move a text placeholder on the slide, rather than mess with text alignment. See "adjust text location" in Chapter 4 for more information.

use numbered lists p. 54

- In the Bullets and Numbering dialog, you can change the starting number of the list, which is handy when you're continuing a list from a previous slide. You can also change the size of the number relative to the text, and change the number's color.

- When you choose a numbering system, pick one that matches the flavor of your presentation. For example, in a formal presentation, you might want to consider using Roman numerals as the numbering system. But that would probably be inappropriate (not to mention pompous) in a presentation about softball teams. Whatever you choose, be consistent from slide to slide; you don't want to use numbers (1, 2, 3...) on one slide and letters (A, B, C...) on the next.

add hyperlinks p. 56

- To remove a hyperlink, select the link, open the Insert Hyperlink dialog, and click the Remove Link button. The text of the link will remain, but it will no longer be a hyperlink.

work with text

6. illustrate your presentation

Images add an important spice to any presentation. Some information is better presented in a graphic form, and often you'll find that your audience will better grasp your message with graphical help. Your presentation can include many different kinds of information that isn't text, such as pictures, charts, diagrams, tables, clip art, sound effects, or video clips. Very few, if any, presentations include all of these elements, but you'll probably want to add at least some to every presentation.

This chapter is where you'll use the images and other media files that you gathered in Chapter 3. If you made a list of files and where they go, find and refer to it as you work through the chapter.

In this chapter, you'll learn how to add images and media clips to your presentation; use PowerPoint's drawing tools to add interest to your slides; and add tables, diagrams, and charts to your presentation.

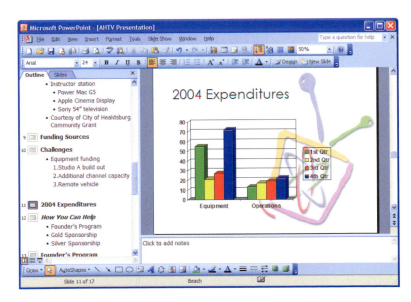

add images from disk

You can add pictures to your PowerPoint presentation by using files on your hard disk or on a CD and inserting them in the presentation.

Display the slide that you want the image on. It should already have a slide layout with a placeholder ready to accept the image. If it doesn't, apply such a layout using the instructions in Chapter 4.

If you used one of the Content layouts in PowerPoint for Windows, click the Insert Picture icon in the Content box.

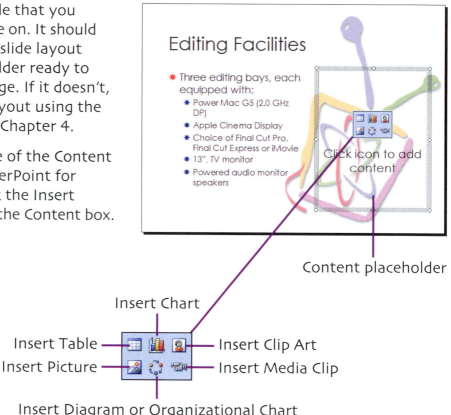

Content placeholder

Insert Chart

Insert Table —— —— Insert Clip Art

Insert Picture —— —— Insert Media Clip

Insert Diagram or Organizational Chart

The Mac version of PowerPoint doesn't use the Content box, so double-click the Picture placeholder.

The Insert Picture (Choose a Picture) dialog appears. Navigate to the picture you want, then click Insert. PowerPoint automatically scales the image to fit inside the placeholder, and the image appears on your slide.

Double click to add picture

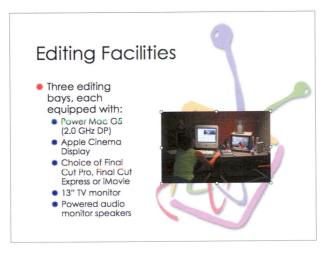

If you don't like the position and size of the image, click on the image and drag it to where you want it to be. Then click one of the selection handles on the image and drag to resize it. As you drag, you'll see a dashed line indicating how large the picture will be when you release the mouse button.

add clip art

Another way to add images to your presentation is by using an image that's in the Clip Organizer (called the Clip Gallery on the Mac).

Display the slide that you want the image on. If it doesn't already have a slide layout with a placeholder ready to accept the image, apply such a layout using the instructions in Chapter 4.

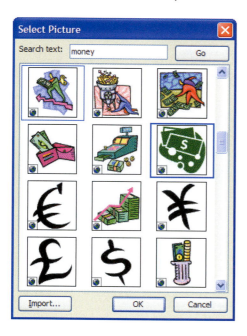

On Windows, click the Insert Clip Art icon in the Content box. The Select Picture dialog will appear. Type a search term into the Search text field and click the Go button.

On the Mac, double-click the Clip Art placeholder. The Clip Gallery will appear. Type a search term into the Search box and click the Search button.

When you find the clip art that you like, click the OK button (Insert button on the Mac). The clip art appears on your slide.

use the drawing tools

If you're the kind of person that can't draw a straight line, much less a circle or an octagon, then PowerPoint's drawing tools are for you. PowerPoint offers tools in the Drawing toolbar (and on the Mac, also in the Add Objects section of the Formatting Palette) with many ready-made shapes that can be easily drawn onto your slides. These AutoShapes include lines, arrows, stars, flowchart symbols, callout boxes, and more.

On Windows, click the AutoShapes pop-up menu on the Drawing toolbar, then choose the shape you want from one of the categories of AutoShapes.

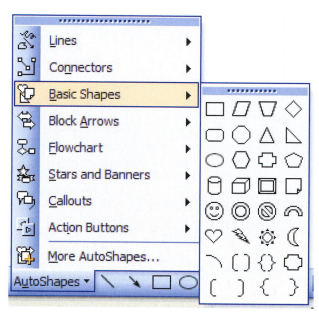

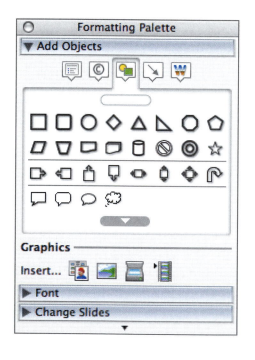

On the Mac, in the Add Objects section of the Formatting Palette, click the AutoShapes tab, then select the shape that you want.

The cursor becomes a cross.

illustrate your presentation

Click and drag on the slide to draw the AutoShape object as large as you wish. Here, I'm using a Cloud callout shape, which serves as a thought bubble for a photo.

Position the drawn AutoShape where you want it, and resize it as needed.

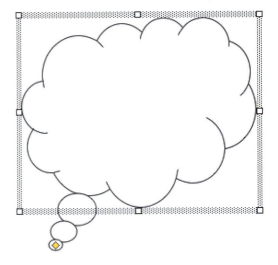

add sound files

Usually, there's no quicker way to annoy your audience than by adding sounds to your slides. It's a big tip-off of novice PowerPoint jockeys. But there are certainly valid reasons for using sounds in presentations. For example, a presentation about music might use brief clips, or anthropologists could include snippets of a language they are studying.

To use a sound, you'll need the sound files to be on your hard disk in a format that your computer can play.

Choose Insert > Movies and Sounds > Sound from File. The Insert Sound dialog appears.

Navigate to the sound file you want, select it, and click OK (Insert).

PowerPoint asks if you want the sound to start automatically when you switch to the slide, or only when you click a button on the slide. Make your choice.

The sound icon appears on the slide. Move it to where you want it. To preview the sound, double-click the sound icon. During the presentation, you will need to click the icon to play the sound, unless you previously told PowerPoint to start the sound automatically.

Sound icon

• Bengal tiger - recorded 9/03

use video clips

Video clips can be very effective in a presentation. You could include a video quote from your product manager, or show a brief tutorial. In the presentation for Access Healdsburg, I used a video clip to take audiences on a tour of the television station's studios.

Video clips must be on your hard disk in a format that your computer can play.

Choose Insert > Movies and Sounds > Movie from File. The Insert Movie dialog appears.

Navigate to the movie file you want, select it, and click OK (Insert).

PowerPoint asks if you want the movie to start automatically when you switch to the slide, or only when you click the movie. Decide which you want.

The movie appears on your slide. You might have to reposition and resize it, especially on a Mac.

Filmstrip icon

If you want to play the movie to preview it, right-click the movie and choose Play Movie from the shortcut menu (Windows) or click the filmstrip icon to display the familiar QuickTime movie controller (Mac). When you give the presentation, click the movie to play it, unless you told PowerPoint to automatically play it when you switched to the slide.

Play button   Movie controller

add diagrams (Win)

PowerPoint for Windows lets you easily insert a variety of predesigned diagrams, such as organization charts and Venn diagrams. You can then customize the diagram for your needs. Here, I've used a radial diagram to show the funding sources for Access Healdsburg. PowerPoint for Mac does not have this feature.

Start by clicking the Insert Diagram or Organization Chart button on the Drawing toolbar.

From the resulting Diagram Gallery dialog, choose the chart that you want.

The diagram appears on the slide, and the Diagram toolbar also appears. This toolbar changes, depending on what sort of diagram you've inserted.

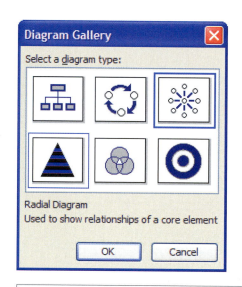

Using the Diagram toolbar, adjust the look of the diagram, changing the number of elements as necessary. For example, I needed more circles in the radial diagram, so I added them.

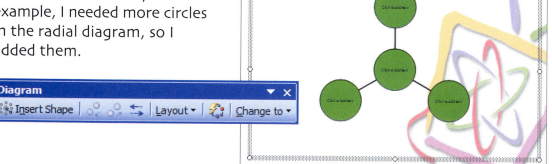

illustrate your presentation

The diagram contains placeholders for text. Click in each one and enter your own text.

Double-click on an element in the diagram to bring up the Format AutoShape dialog to change its coloring. The resulting diagram gets the message across.

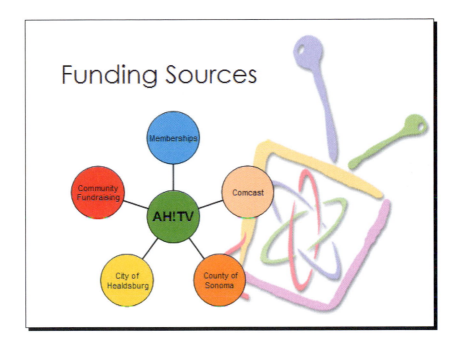

add charts

Many slide presentations include a set of numbers of some kind—for example, projected fundraising for next year, or a look back at last year's budget versus actual numbers. It's difficult for an audience to understand long columns of numbers, especially in the short time they would be on the screen during your presentation. A chart offers a much better way to let people quickly grasp the relationship between numbers and helps them spot trends.

Insert Chart

To add a chart to one of your slides, start by clicking the Insert Chart button on the Standard toolbar.

On the Mac, a new program, Microsoft Graph, starts up, displaying a new menu bar, a new set of toolbars, a datasheet where you enter data to be charted, and a preview of the chart. The datasheet is already populated with some sample data for you.

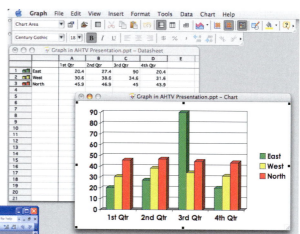

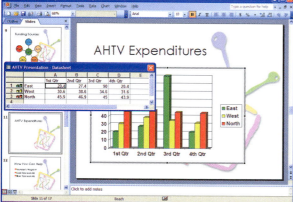

On Windows, Graph takes over the PowerPoint window.

illustrate your presentation

Change the sample data in the datasheet one cell at a time, entering your own data. As you change the datasheet, the chart preview automatically updates.

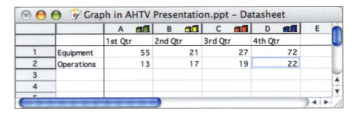

Use the Graph toolbars to make any other changes you need in the chart, such as changing the chart type, chart colors, and so on.

On Windows, click the slide background to close Graph and return to PowerPoint. On the Mac, choose Graph > Quit and Return to [presentation name]. The new chart appears on your slide.

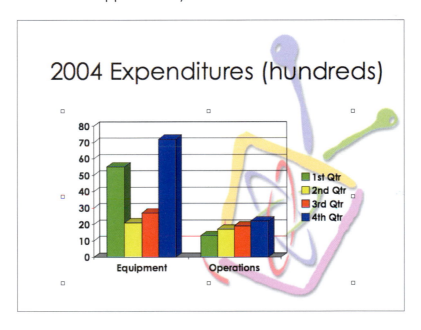

add tables

Tables are a great way to show relationships between groups of data, and to get a lot of information into your presentation in an easy-to-understand fashion. Tables can contain words, numbers, or both.

On the Standard toolbar, click Insert Table. The table grid appears. Drag to select the number of rows and columns that you need in your table.

When you click, a blank table is inserted into the current slide.

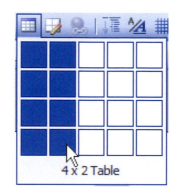

If you want, point at the horizontal or vertical lines inside the table until the cursor turns into a double-headed arrow. Then click and drag to resize the rows or columns.

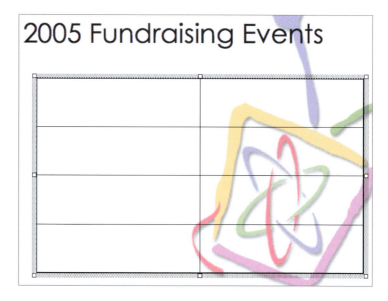

2005 Fundraising Events

illustrate your presentation

Click inside the first cell of the table to get an insertion point, then enter your data into the cells. You can press the Tab key to move between cells without using the mouse. When you're finished adding data to the table, click on the slide background to deselect the table.

2005 Fundraising Events

Q1	Winter Telethon
Q2	Spring Carnival
Q3	Harvest Time Telethon
Q4	Halloween Dinner & Ball

extra bits

add images from disk p. 64

- You can also add an image to a slide by dragging and dropping it from the desktop onto your slide. Sometimes this is faster than navigating through the Open dialog, but the disadvantage to dragging and dropping (as opposed to using a placeholder to insert the image) is that you'll have to resize the image yourself.

- Got a picture that's not as clear as you wish it could be? You can change the brightness and contrast of images that you import by double-clicking them to bring up the Format Picture dialog. Click the Picture tab, then use the Brightness and Contrast sliders to adjust the picture. Click the Preview button to see the effect on the image. When you're happy with the result, click OK.

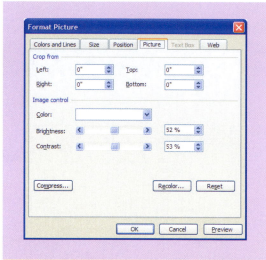

add clip art p. 66

- You can also store photographs and media clips, not just line art, in the Clip Organizer (Clip Gallery).

use the drawing tools p. 68

- You can layer text and graphics, so if you want to, for example, put text inside a callout Auto-Shape, you would insert a Text Box over the callout shape.

- You can add colors to an AutoShape by double-clicking it, and then using the Fill and Line controls in the resulting Format AutoShapes dialog.

- The Mac has a Drawing toolbar, too; choose View > Toolbars > Drawing to display it. In fact, you'll find more drawing options in the Drawing toolbar than in the Formatting Palette.

- If you need to precisely line up objects, you'll find alignment and distribution commands in the Draw pop-up menu on the Drawing toolbar.

add sound files p. 70

- On Windows, PowerPoint can use the following kinds of sound files: AIFF, AU, MIDI, MP3, Windows Audio file (WAV), and Windows Media Audio file (WMA). On the Mac, Power-Point supports any audio type that QuickTime supports, including AAC, AIFF, AU, MIDI, MOV, MP3, SFIL, and WAV.

- Depending on your presentation setting, it can be effective to attach a music file to the first and last slides of your presentation, which helps introduce and end the show.

- You'll find additional sound effects in the Clip Organizer on Windows.

use video clips p. 71

- On Windows, PowerPoint can use the following kinds of video files: Windows Media file (ASF), Windows Video file (AVI), MPEG, and Windows Media Video files (WMV). On the Mac, PowerPoint supports any video type that QuickTime supports, including AVI, DV, Flash (SWF), MPEG, and MOV.

illustrate your presentation

extra bits

add diagrams (Win) p. 72

- You can add an organizational chart on a Mac, though you don't get the other nice predesigned diagrams. Choose Insert > Picture > Organization Chart. A separate program, Microsoft Organization Chart, opens and lets you create and adjust the org chart. When you're done, close the program, and the new org chart is automatically pasted into your PowerPoint slide.

add charts p. 74

- Besides entering chart data directly in PowerPoint's datasheet, you can also copy and paste spreadsheet data from Microsoft Excel into the datasheet.

- If you're more comfortable working with charts in Excel, you can create a chart in Excel, copy it, then paste it into a PowerPoint slide.

add tables p. 76

- When you're editing a table, the Tables and Borders toolbar appears. You can use this toolbar to draw new lines in your table; erase existing lines; add a fill color to table cells; and change the thickness of the lines in the table. It also contains two handy buttons to help you resize rows and columns: Distribute Rows Evenly and Distribute Columns Evenly.

illustrate your presentation

7. make it move

Your presentation is nearly complete. You've written the content, chosen a design, set the layout of each slide, and added images and media files. The last major task before you give the presentation is to give it some movement, by adding slide transitions and slide effects.

Slide transitions are the animated effects the audience sees when you switch from one slide to the next in the presentation. PowerPoint provides many different transition effects, and you've probably seen them all (even the really tasteless ones). Slide effects are animations that occur within a slide. For example, you can have each bullet point fade onto the screen as you get to it, and then dim to gray text as you move to the next point. Or you can have an image, graph, or diagram glide onto the screen.

In this chapter, you'll rearrange the order of your slides in the Slide Sorter View and then set slide transitions and effects.

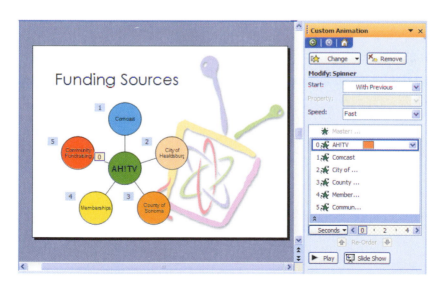

rearrange slides

As you've been developing your presentation, you've seen how the topic of one slide flows into the next, and perhaps that flow is perfect for your show. But maybe the presentation would be a bit better, a touch tighter, if you moved that slide there, and moved that other slide over here. PowerPoint's Slide Sorter View shows you many slides at once, and allows you to drag one or more slides to other places in the presentation. Slide Sorter View also offers a convenient way to apply slide transitions and slide effects to multiple slides in one operation (you'll see how to do that in the next section).

To enter Slide Sorter View, choose View > Slide Sorter, or click the Slide Sorter View button at the bottom of the PowerPoint window.

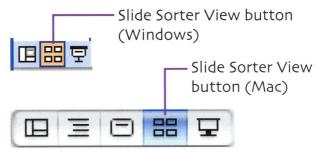

Slide Sorter View button (Windows)

Slide Sorter View button (Mac)

In Slide Sorter View, you see thumbnail views of the slides; the currently selected slide shows a darker border around it.

Selected slide

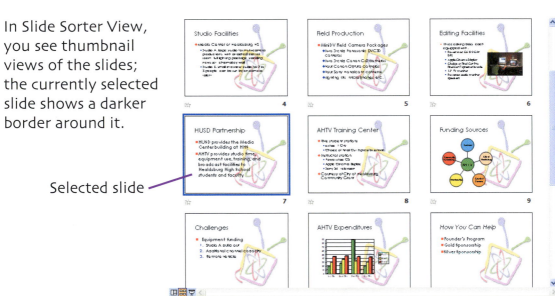

To move a slide, click on the slide you want to move, then drag it to the new location. As you drag, an indicator line will show you where the slide will go when you release the mouse button.

┌─ Slide indicator line ◄············

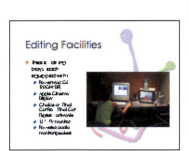

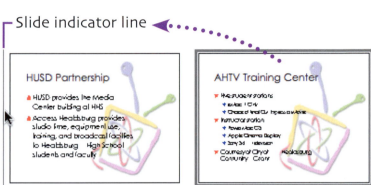

6   7   8

set slide transitions

Transitions between slides can enhance your presentation's message and add visual interest to your show. You can add transitions to one or more slides at one time in either the Normal or Slide Sorter View (though I find it's usually easier to use Slide Sorter View). PowerPoint includes dozens of special transition effects to choose from, ranging from subtle to the polar opposite of subtle. With slide transitions, as with any animation in PowerPoint, you should live by the principle "less is more" when choosing transitions, because the flashier they are, the more quickly your audience will become tired of them.

1 Switch to Slide Sorter View to begin setting the transition; choose View > Slide Sorter.

2 Select the slides to which you want to apply the transitions. To select multiple slides, click on the first slide, hold down the Shift key, and click the last slide. Those slides and all slides in between are selected.

3 Choose Slide Show > Slide Transition.

On Windows, the Slide Transition Task Pane opens.

Transition list ——

Transition speed ——

Sound pop-up menu ——

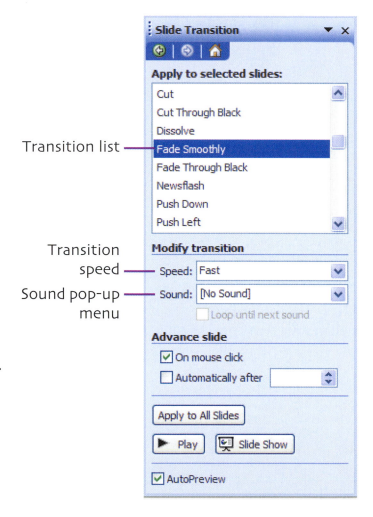

make it move

On the Mac, the Slide
Transition dialog appears.

Transition pop-up menu —

Preview area —

Transition speed —

Sound pop-up menu —

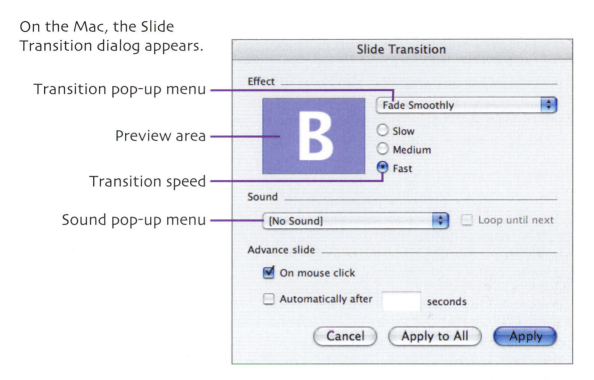

4 On Windows, choose a transition effect from the transition list which applies the effect. If the AutoPreview setting at the bottom of the Task Pane is checked, you'll see a preview of the effect on the slide thumbnails in the Slide Sorter.

On the Mac, choose the transition effect from the transition pop-up menu. You'll see the effect in the preview area of the dialog.

5 Choose the speed of the transition by selecting it from the Speed pop-up menu (Windows) or clicking one of the Speed radio buttons (Mac).

6 If you want, choose a sound from the Sound pop-up menu. This sound will play between each of the selected slides. Use this sparingly; many audiences hate sound effects in presentations.

7 Click Apply to add the transition to the selected slides, or click Apply to All Slides (Apply to All) to add the transition to the entire presentation.

make it move

set slide effects (Win)

You've seen slide effects in most presentations; these are the effects that are responsible for titles, bulleted text, charts, or diagrams that fade, wipe, or animate onto the screen when the presenter clicks the mouse button. PowerPoint for Windows has two ways to apply animation to objects on your slides. The first way is to use animation schemes, which are preset animations that are easy to apply. The other way is to create a custom animation, where you're in complete control of each of the elements on the slide.

To apply an animation scheme, first choose View > Normal, then display the slide to which you want to apply the animation scheme. Next, choose Slide Show > Animation Schemes. The Animation Schemes Task Pane opens.

The scheme list is divided into categories: Subtle, Moderate, and Exciting, in rough order of how extreme the scheme is. At the subtle end, a scheme such as Wipe makes the title fade onto the screen, then each bullet point wipes onto the screen from left to right. At the extreme end, the motion sickness-inducing Neutron scheme makes each letter in the title spiral in an orbit to its final destination, then each bullet point slides up from the bottom of the screen. Ick. Unless you have a very specific reason, I suggest you stick with the schemes in the Subtle category.

Click on a scheme in the scheme list. The slide pane shows you a preview of the animation. To play it again, click the Play button at the bottom of the Task Pane. If you're happy with the effect, click Apply to All Slides, and the entire presentation will take on the animation scheme.

make it move

add custom animation

Sometimes animation schemes don't really do the trick; you need more control over moving items on or off the screen, or you want to apply an animated effect to a particular part of the slide. For example, in the Access Healdsburg presentation, the Funding Sources slide contains a diagram that can be enhanced with a little animation. PowerPoint for Windows has a terrific custom animation capability.

Because I'm going to talk about each of the funding sources, I'll build up the diagram a bubble at a time, starting with the green center bubble (which will appear on the screen first), then adding each of the source bubbles, beginning at the top and moving clockwise. Each bubble will appear after I click the mouse.

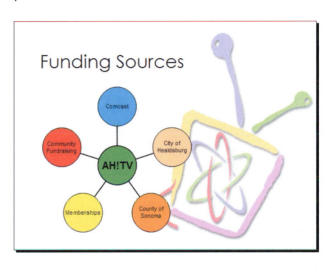

Begin by choosing Slide Show > Custom Animation, which opens the Custom Animation Task Pane.

Animation list ⎯⎯⎯

Select the first element you want to animate; I chose the center bubble in the diagram.

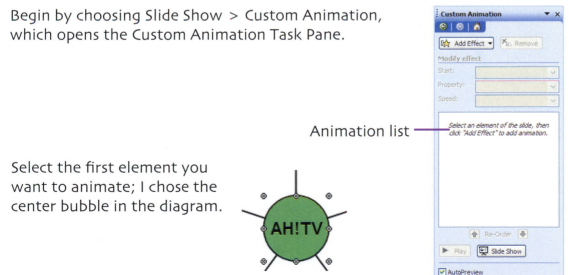

add custom animation

The Add Effect button in the Task Pane is really a pop-up menu; choose an effect from the Entrance category (because you're animating how the element will be entering the slide; if you want the element to fly off the screen later, you can add an effect from the Exit category). I chose Spinner, which fades up the element while spinning it.

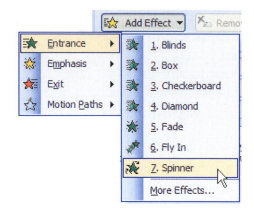

The effect preview shows that the entire diagram spins onto the screen, which isn't what we want; we want each bubble in the diagram to appear separately. A look at the animation list shows that the whole diagram is set to animate.

To split the elements of the diagram so that we can animate each one separately, right-click the item in the animation list, and choose Effect Options.

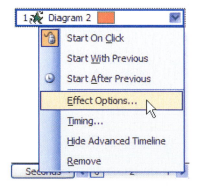

In the resulting Spinner dialog, click the Diagram Animation tab, then make a choice from the drop-down menu. I want the center bubble to appear first, followed by each bubble moving clockwise, so I chose Clockwise – Outward. Click OK.

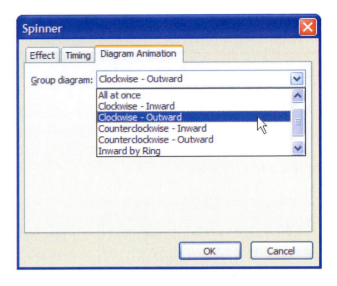

Each element of the diagram is now numbered separately, and the animation list contains an entry for each element. If you want, you can now add a separate animation effect for each element. Just right-click each element in the animation list and make changes.

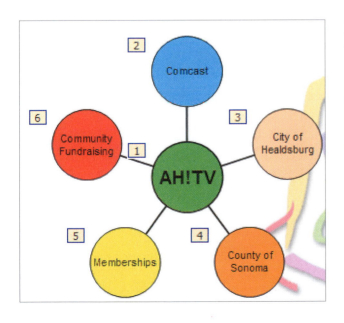

set slide effects (Mac)

Like its Windows sibling, PowerPoint for Mac gives you two ways to control slide effects. Preset animations apply simple animations to the elements on the slide; custom animation gives you more control over each element (though not, alas, as much control as PowerPoint for Windows).

To use a preset animation, first choose View > Normal, then display the slide to which you want to apply the preset. Next, choose Slide Show > Preset Animations, then choose a preset from the cascading menu. The animation is applied to the slide.

Custom animations are a bit more complex to apply, but are much more flexible.

1 Begin by choosing View > Normal, then display the slide to which you want to apply the animation.

2 Choose Slide Show > Custom Animation. The Custom Animation dialog appears.

Preview pane

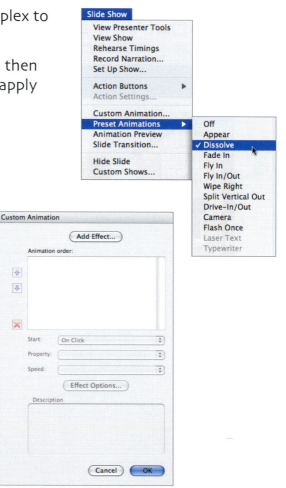

3 In the Select to animate list, which contains the elements of the slide that can be animated, select the element you want to animate.

4 Click Add Effect. The Animation Effects dialog appears. It is divided into four categories: Basic, Subtle, Moderate, and Exciting. It's a good idea to stick to items in the Basic or Subtle category; it's better for the audience. I chose a wipe effect for the bulleted text on my slides.

As you click an effect, you can see its result in the Preview pane of the Custom Animation dialog.

The elements appear in the Animation order list, and the animation controls become active.

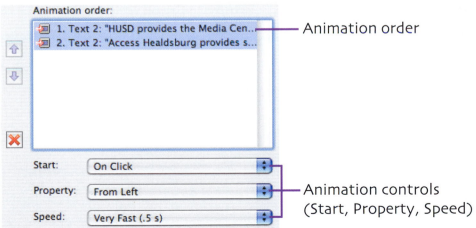

Animation order

Animation controls
(Start, Property, Speed)

set slide effects (Mac)

In this case, I want to change the wipe direction from From Bottom to From Left, so the text appears in the same way that people read. I choose this in the Property pop-up menu (this menu changes depending on the kind of effect you've set, so it may not look exactly like the one shown).

You can also change when the animation starts and its speed, from Very Slow (5 seconds) to Very Fast (.5 second), or you can set a custom time.

5 Click OK to apply the custom animation.

extra bits

rearrange slides p. 82

- If you want to move a group of slides at one time, in Slide Sorter View, click on the first slide, hold down the Shift key, and click the last slide. Those two slides and all slides in between will be selected, and you can drag and drop them as a group.

set slide transitions p. 84

- You can also select multiple slides in the Slide Sorter by clicking in a blank space between slides, then dragging over the slides you want.

- By default, PowerPoint is set so that the transition is triggered when you click the mouse during your presentation. But you can use the settings in the Advance slide section of the Slide Transition Task Pane to set the slide to automatically change to the next slide after a given number of seconds.

- Windows users have it a little better than Mac users when it comes to setting transitions. The Slide Transition Task Pane not only allows you to preview transition effects with thumbnails of the actual slides, but you can also use the Play button

to trigger the preview manually, and the Slide Show button puts PowerPoint into Slide Show mode, allowing you to see the slides and transitions full screen.

Mac users must apply a transition, then test it in the Slide Show or the small Animation Preview window.

To open the Animation Preview

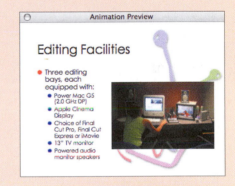

window, choose Slide Show > Animation Preview. Click anywhere in the window to see the preview play.

- You can purchase add-ins (programs that extend PowerPoint) that give you additional slide transitions beyond the ones that come with PowerPoint. One well-known maker of these add-ins is Crystal Graphics (www.crystalgraphics.com), with their PowerPlugs series.

extra bits

set slide effects (Win) p. 86

- If you're having problems controlling when images on your slides appear, it's probably because the image is using an image placeholder. The placeholder is part of the slide's master, and it can't be changed with the animation controls. The solution is to select the image, then choose Edit > Cut. The picture will disappear, and the placeholder will appear. Select the placeholder, then press Backspace (Delete) to get rid of it. Finally, choose Edit > Paste to bring back the picture. Now the picture is in the same layer as the rest of the slide elements, and it will respond to the animation controls.

add custom animation p. 87

- The choices in the Effect Options dialog will be different, depending on what you have selected. For example, if you're animating bulleted text, there will be a Text Animation tab in the dialog.

- You can change the timing for each element in the animation list separately. The orange bar in the list is the length of the animation for that element.

To change the length of the element's animation, point at the orange bar. The cursor will change to a double-headed arrow. Click and drag the bar to the desired length.

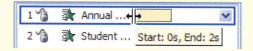

- PowerPoint for Windows can create and play animations that the Mac version can't match, including animation of elements along paths, and it has many more effects from which to choose. Motion path animation effects created in PowerPoint for Windows will play in PowerPoint 2004 for Mac, but not in earlier versions. Custom animations of diagrams created on Windows will not play in PowerPoint for Mac; the diagram will appear, but without its animation.

　　　　　　　　　　make it move

set slide effects
(Mac) p. 90

- To apply preset animations to all the slides in your presentation in one operation, switch to Slide Sorter View, and choose Edit > Select All or press Cmd-A. Then choose the preset animation from the Slide Show menu.

- Click the Effect Options button in the Custom Animation dialog to get more precise control over effects, timing, and specific animation controls for the selected kind of slide element.

make it move

8. prepare to present

Now that you've finished putting together your presentation, there are some things you can do to make it better before you step on stage. The easiest way to improve your talk is familiar to anyone who has done any kind of performance: Rehearse it before you get in front of your audience. You can also send your presentation to co-workers for their comments; it's amazing how often other people will suggest a great point that you missed.

To help you give the presentation, you can create and print speaker notes, and to help the audience, you can print handouts containing your slides. In this chapter, you'll see how a little final preparation can help make your presentation a smashing success.

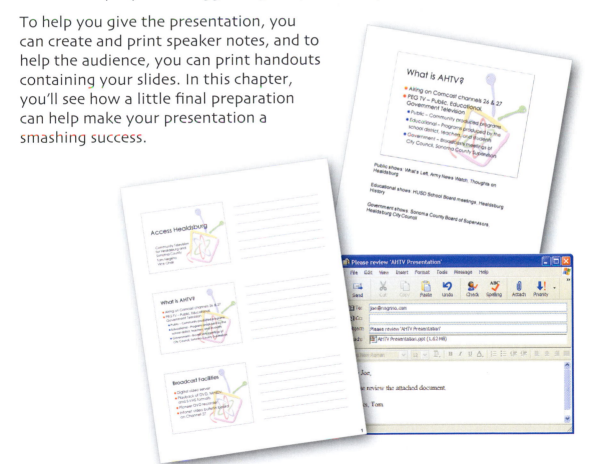

get colleague review

One easy way to improve your presentation is to show it to other people for their comments. You'll often gain valuable insights into your presentation by getting this feedback. I've had some co-workers suggest areas that I should have mentioned, and others give me some great images that I incorporated into my show. If possible, allow people to watch you rehearse, then solicit their constructive criticism. Believe me, your final presentation will be better for it.

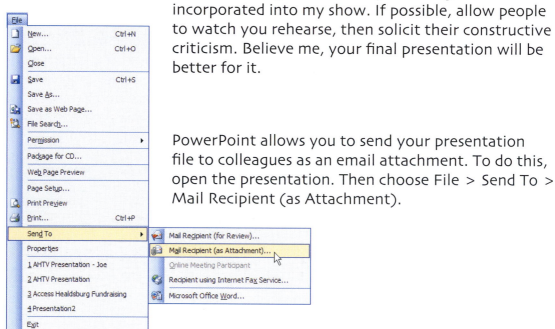

PowerPoint allows you to send your presentation file to colleagues as an email attachment. To do this, open the presentation. Then choose File > Send To > Mail Recipient (as Attachment).

Your email program will open and create a new message with a subject filled in and the file attached. Address the email, enter a note for your recipient, and click Send.

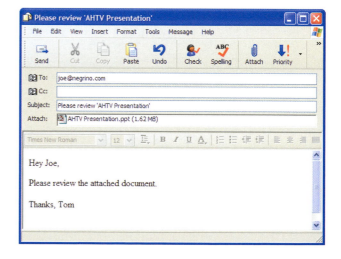

rehearse your show

Rehearsals are key to any production, whether it is a Broadway play, a concert, or your slide show. When you rehearse your presentation, you get a better feel for what you want to say to accompany the slides, and it helps you make sure that you stay within your allotted time. Being able to do the whole presentation at your own pace is infinitely preferable to trying to stretch if you run short, or worse, getting the hook if you run too long. Unless you have a lot of experience presenting, rehearsal is the best way to find out how long your presentation really is.

PowerPoint has a built-in rehearsal feature that can tell you how long you spend on each slide, and when you're done, it will tell you the total time for the presentation.

Choose Slide Show > Rehearse Timings. The slide show appears full-screen, covering up everything else on your monitor.

On Windows, the Rehearsal toolbar appears.

On the Mac, you get a small timer that changes for each slide. Clicking the timer advances the presentation to the next slide or next slide effect, the same as clicking the mouse.

rehearse your show (cont.)

Give the presentation for each slide. To trigger the next slide effect or to advance to the next slide, click the mouse button or press the right arrow key on the keyboard. When you are done with the presentation, PowerPoint displays a dialog asking if you are happy with the slide timings, and if you want it to store them for future use. If you want, PowerPoint can use these timings to advance your presentation automatically when you give it, rather than you advancing it manually.

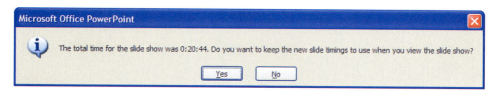

If you click yes, PowerPoint for Windows drops you into Slide Sorter mode, where you can review the timing for each slide. On the Mac, PowerPoint asks if you want to go to the Slide Sorter. You can see a variety of information about each slide in the Slide Sorter.

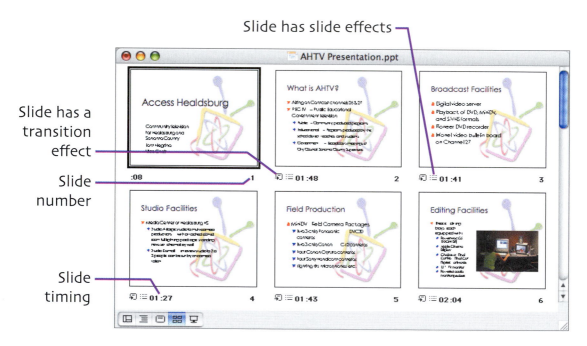

create speaker notes

Speaker Notes are printed notes that you'll use to help keep you on track while you're giving the presentation. As you saw way back in Chapter 1, PowerPoint has an area in Normal view where you can type in your notes for each slide.

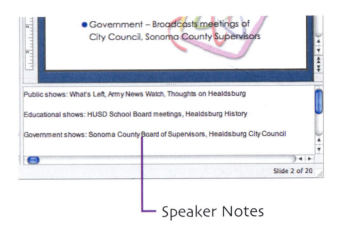

Speaker Notes

These notes don't appear on the presentation screen, but if you're using a laptop to present with an external projector or monitor, the notes will appear on the laptop screen, so you can see them, but your audience can't.

If you prefer, you can also print Speaker Notes (let's say that you won't be operating the computer yourself) so that you can refer to notes without being tethered to your computer. When PowerPoint prints Speaker Notes, they appear one slide to a page, with your notes underneath.

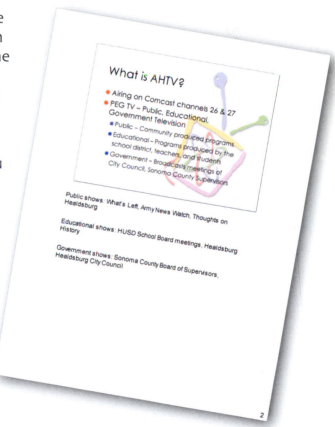

print speaker notes

To print the Speaker Notes, choose File > Print. From the Print what pop-up menu, choose Notes Pages (on the Mac, Notes), then click OK (on the Mac, click Print).

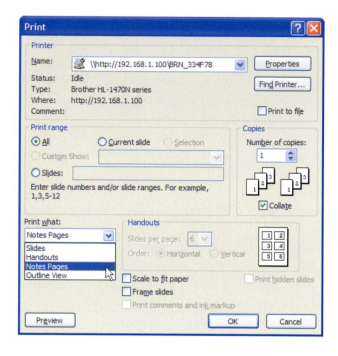

print slides & handouts

You can print slides and handouts for your use (or the audience's) in color (with a color printer, of course), grayscale, or black and white. When you print slides, just the slide appears on the page, filling the page, in landscape format (meaning the slide is rotated so that the wide side of the slide is aligned with the length of the printed page).

For handouts, PowerPoint gives you a choice of 1, 2, 3, 4, 6, or 9 slides per printed page, shrinking the slides to fit. If you want your audience to be able to take notes easily, I suggest that you use the 3-slides-per-page option; it's the only one that provides lines next to the slides for audience notes, and the slides are a good size for easy readibility.

To print slides, choose File > Print. In the Print dialog, choose Slides from the Print what pop-up menu. From the Color/grayscale (on the Mac it's called Output) pop-up menu, decide how you want the page to print. If you choose Grayscale or Pure Black and White, the background of the slide will not print. Click OK (Print) to print the slides.

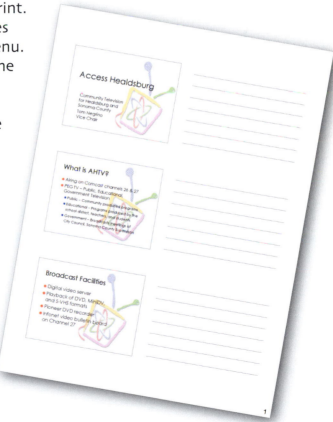

print slides & handouts

To print handouts in Windows, choose File > Print. In the Print dialog, choose Handouts from the Print what pop-up menu. The handouts section of the Print dialog will become active. Choose the number of slides per handout page you want (a preview icon gives you an idea what the layout will look like). Make a choice from the Color/grayscale pop-up menu, then click OK to print the handouts.

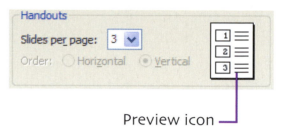

Preview icon

To print handouts on the Mac, choose File > Print. In the Print dialog, choose Handouts from the Print What pop-up menu. A preview of the page appears in the Quick Preview area on the left side of the dialog. Make a color choice from the Output pop-up menu, then click Print to print the handouts.

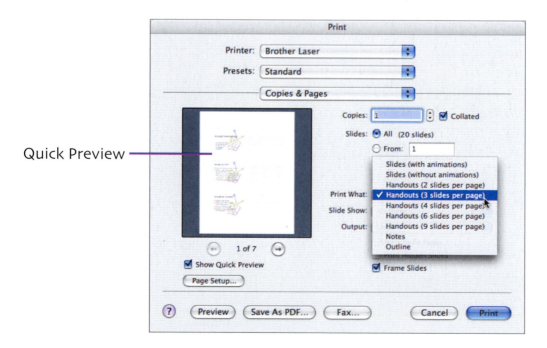

Quick Preview

extra bits

get colleague review p. 98

- If your co-worker doesn't have PowerPoint installed on his or her machine, you have a few options. You could, for example, print the presentation, then send your colleague the paper. But if you want to send a file via email, you need to get the file into a format that can be easily read, such as PDF (Portable Document Format), which can be read by the free Adobe Reader on most operating systems, and also by Preview on the Mac.

  Mac users have it easy; they can print any file, including a PowerPoint file, to PDF simply by clicking the Save As PDF button at the bottom of the Print dialog. Windows users don't have this built-in PDF facility. If you want to print to PDF, I suggest that you look into Macromedia FlashPaper 2 ($79), which allows you to print any file in either PDF format or as a Macromedia Flash file. FlashPaper 2 even has plug-ins for Microsoft Office that allow you to easily convert any Office file to PDF or Flash.

- PowerPoint for Windows has a better (but more complex) way to get and incorporate reviewer's comments than the Mac version. You can save a presentation in a special format called "Presentation for Review," after which you send the presentation to others. They can then make changes to the file and email it back to you. When you open it, you can merge their changes with your original presentation file. Detailing this review process is beyond the scope of this book; to learn how to do it, choose Help > Microsoft Office PowerPoint Help, then search for "review." Click the topic "About sending a presentation for review."

rehearse your show p. 99

- When you're rehearsing timings, it's a good idea to speak your narration just as you would during the presentation. Stand up or sit up straight, breathe normally, and speak clearly without rushing.

extra bits

print slides & handouts p. 103

- The choice of 1 slide per handout is only available on PowerPoint for Windows.

- On the Mac, you have the option of printing slides with or without animations. If you print with animations, you will get as many slides printed as you have slide effects. For example, let's say you have a slide with a title and three bullet points. The bullet points wipe onto the screen one by one. Printing the slide with animations means that you'll get four pages, one for the slide with just the title, and then one more page for each bullet point. Most of the time, you'll want to print slides without animations.

9. deliver your presentation

Finally, you're ready to give your presentation. You've arrived at the room where you'll give the talk, and perhaps the audience is beginning to arrive. You need to connect your notebook computer to the projector, set up your computer so that it recognizes the two displays (the notebook screen and the projector), and run the show.

If you don't have a notebook, and you know that the presentation venue will have a computer and projector waiting for you, you can burn your presentation to a CD and just bring that. See Chapter 10 for how to burn a CD of your presentation.

During the presentation, you can use PowerPoint's Presenter Tools, which allow you to control your show and to display your Speaker Notes as you present, using an interface that only you see. You can also annotate your slides and make additional notes during the presentation.

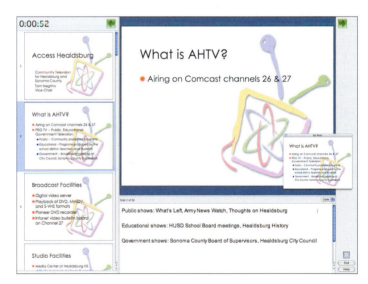

set up projector (Win)

You'll typically want to deliver a presentation with a notebook computer connected to a projector or large monitor. Your computer must support multiple monitors. To use multiple monitors on Windows, you must be running Windows XP (or Windows 2000 SP3 or later). Your notebook must also have a VGA video output (most do). You'll view the presentation on your notebook screen, and your audience will view the projected screen.

First, turn off the projector and computer.

Hook the projector (if you don't have a projector, you can use another external display, such as a monitor) up to the notebook. Most PC notebooks have a VGA port, but some require an adapter; check the documentation for your notebook.

Turn on the projector and the computer. The notebook should recognize the existence of a second display. To configure your computer for multiple monitors, right-click the desktop, then choose Properties from the shortcut menu. The Display Properties dialog will open. Click the Settings tab.

The two monitors will appear as icons in the dialog. The notebook screen is always the primary monitor (labeled with a 1), by default.

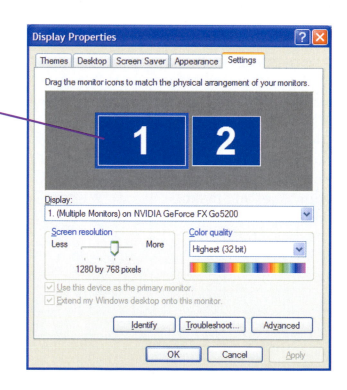

deliver your presentation

Click the icon for the second monitor, click "Extend my Windows desktop onto this monitor," and then click Apply. The second monitor should now show your desktop wallpaper. Click OK to save your settings.

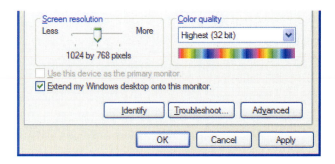

Now that you are set up for multiple monitors, you need to tell PowerPoint that you'll be using a projector. Open your presentation in PowerPoint, then choose Slide Show > Set Up Show. In the Multiple monitors section, choose the projector from the "Display slide show on" pop-up menu.

If you want to use the Presenter View, click the Show Presenter View checkbox, then click OK. To learn more about Presenter View, see use presenter view, later in this chapter.

set up projector (Mac)

Setting up dual-display mode and hooking up a projector to a Mac is straight-forward; just follow these steps.

First, turn off the projector and computer.

Hook the projector up to the Mac. Apple notebooks usually need an adapter to connect their VGA output to the projector's VGA input. Older iBooks, iBook G4, and 12" PowerBook G4 machines use the Apple mini-DVI-to-VGA adapter; the 15" and 17" PowerBook G4 machines use the Apple DVI-to-VGA adapter. All of these machines come with their respective adapters. The older Titanium PowerBook G4 notebooks have a VGA port, so they don't need an adapter.

Turn on the projector and the computer. The Mac will recognize the existence of a second display and will go into mirrored mode, which puts the same image on the external display as is on the notebook's screen. Open System Preferences and choose Displays. In the Displays dialog, click the Display tab. Two windows will appear, one for each display.

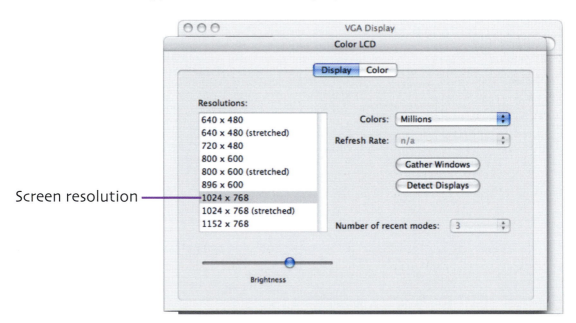

Click the screen resolution that matches the resolution of the projector. It will typically be either 800 X 600 or 1024 X 768. The two mirrored screens will change to the selected resolution.

If you don't want to use PowerPoint's Presenter Tools, your setup is done. To use Presenter Tools, you'll need to take the displays out of mirrored mode and into extended desktop mode, where the projector and notebook screen become one continuous desktop. If your Mac doesn't support extended desktop mode (iBooks, for example, only do mirroring), you can't use Presenter Tools.

Open System Preferences and choose Displays. In the Displays dialog, click the Arrangement tab, then clear the Mirror Displays checkbox.

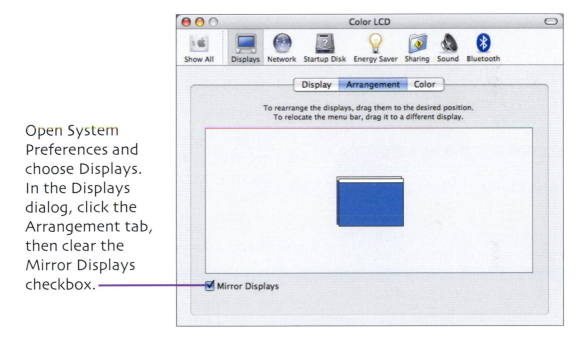

You can now set the resolution for each display separately. Click on the Display tab for each of the two display windows, and click the desired resolution.

prepare yourself

So now you have created a terrific presentation, your notebook and the projector are set up, and your audience is beginning to drift into the room, eager for the show. But what about you? What about your needs? If you're like most people, you're feeling a little stage fright at this point. Dealing with your butterflies is what this section is about. Here are some tips that can help you keep your presentation running smoothly.

- If you can, get to the presentation venue early. Sit or stand where you will be speaking, and make sure that your seating (or the podium) is adjusted the way that you want it. Take a moment to adjust the microphone (if any) and work with the venue's audio technician to get the levels right before the audience arrives. Make sure you have a spot to place a cup of water. Getting comfortable with the physical space and facilities helps a lot.

- If you have the opportunity to greet some of the audience members as they enter the room, you should do so. It's easier to speak to people you know, even if all you've done is said hello.

- Before you begin, visualize yourself giving a successful presentation. Imagine that you've spoken very well, and hear your audience's applause. Picture audience members coming up to congratulate you after the show. It sounds a bit silly, but visualizing success works.

- Concentrate on your message, not on the audience. If you focus on what you're saying, you will distract yourself from being nervous.

- If you are nervous, never apologize for it. Except in extreme cases, most audiences don't notice that speakers are nervous, and it doesn't help your case to point it out.

- Always keep in mind that your audience wants you to succeed. People don't go to a presentation thinking, "I sure hope this guy does a lousy talk and wastes my time." They want to get something out of your presentation as much as you do.

- Unless you are a professional comedian, keep the jokes to a minimum, or skip them altogether. A joke that falls flat isn't a good way to start a show.

- Never read straight from a script. Very few people can read from a script without putting their audience to sleep; we call those few people actors.

- Don't read your slides aloud word for word. Your slides should be signposts and reminders of what you want to say. Using your slides as a teleprompter is another way to lose audience interest. If you need prompting for your topics, use your Speaker Notes.

- After the presentation is over, thank your audience and make yourself available for questions. Make sure to get feedback from them so that you can improve your next show.

run the presentation

To run the presentation, choose View > Slide Show, or click the Slide Show button at the lower-left corner of the PowerPoint window. On Windows, you can also press F5 on your keyboard.

Slide Show button (Windows)   Slide Show button (Mac)

The presentation appears on the screen. If you are using a projector or external monitor, the presentation appears on whichever screen you selected during setup.

During the presentation, if you're not using the Presenter View (Presenter Tools), PowerPoint provides some onscreen tools that you can use to control your show. They include ways to move to the previous and next slides, a menu that allows you to jump to any slide or custom show in your presentation, and a way to pause your presentation or turn the screen black for a moment.

These controls appear at the bottom-left corner of the screen when you move the pointer over them. On Windows, they are unobtrusive icons.

Previous slide ———  ——— Next slide

Control menu

On the Mac, there is a pop-up menu with the controls; click the menu's icon to bring up the pop-up menu.

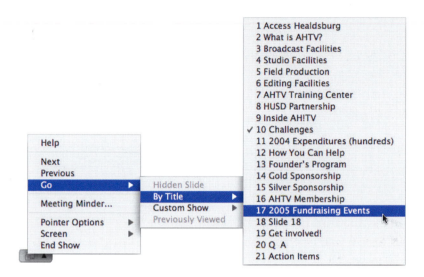

To advance to the next slide or slide effect, click the mouse button, or press the Right Arrow key on the keyboard. To return to a previous slide, press the Left Arrow key.

At the end of the show, PowerPoint for Windows will go to a black screen; click the mouse button to leave Slide Show mode and go back to the Power-Point window. On the Mac, you drop out of Slide Show mode and go back to the PowerPoint window automatically when you advance past the last slide. To end the slide show manually, press the Esc key on your keyboard.

use presenter view

Presenter View (called Presenter Tools on the Mac) is a new feature that gives you more control over the presentation as you are giving it. It gives you a control panel that you see on your notebook's screen, while the audience sees the regular slide show on the projector.

This mode is only available when you are using multiple monitors on Windows; on the Mac, choosing View > Presenter Tools allows you to use the Presenter Tools to rehearse your presentation without a second display.

In Presenter View, you get a scrolling list of your slide thumbnails, a large view of the current slide, buttons for Previous Slide and Next Slide, your Speaker Notes, and best of all, an onscreen timer that tells you the elapsed time of your presentation. This timer is a great tool to help you stay on track; by knowing how long you have been talking, you can speed up or slow down to keep within your allotted speaking time.

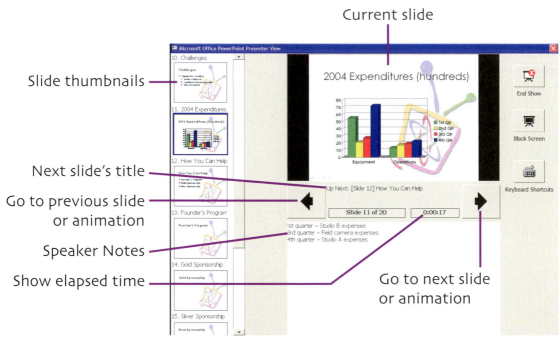

Presenter View for Windows

deliver your presentation

On the Mac, Presenter Tools works in much the same way, except that you get a small floating Up Next window that shows you the upcoming slide or slide animation effect.

Presenter Tools for Mac

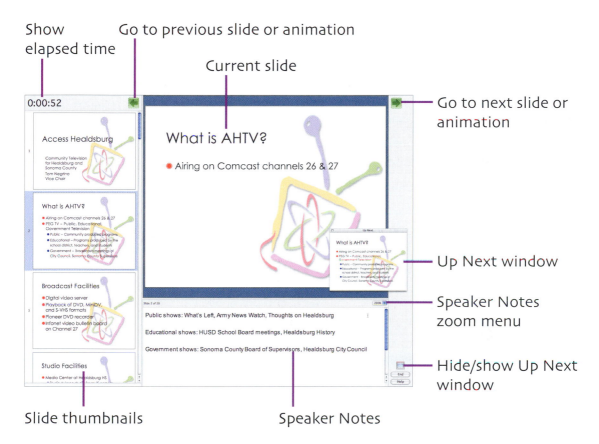

Show elapsed time

Go to previous slide or animation

Current slide

Go to next slide or animation

Up Next window

Speaker Notes zoom menu

Hide/show Up Next window

Slide thumbnails

Speaker Notes

To jump ahead to any slide in your presentation, scroll the list of slide thumbnails, then click the slide you want. If there is a slide transition associated with the slide you clicked, it will trigger and the slide will appear on the projector.

create custom shows

Have you ever needed to show part of a presentation, but not all of it, for a particular audience? For example, let's say that you have a presentation about a new product that includes slides with commission rates for the sales department. When you give the presentation to the marketing department, you can omit the commission slides by creating a custom show. This is a subset of the presentation that includes just the slides you want. To create a custom show, open your presentation, then choose Slide Show > Custom Shows. The Custom Shows dialog appears.

Click the New button, and in the Define Custom Show dialog, name the custom show, then select slides from the list on the left, and click the Add button to add them to the list on the right.

Click OK, and then, back in the Custom Shows dialog, click Close.

To run the custom show, choose Slide Show > Set Up Show. In the Show slides section of the resulting dialog, click Custom show, and then choose the show you want from the pop-up menu. Click OK. When you run the presentation, the custom show will run.

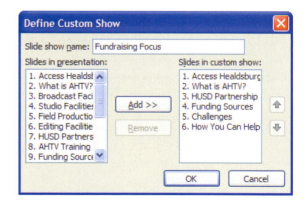

extra bits

set up projector (Win) p. 108

- If you're not sure which monitor is which, click the Identify button in the Settings tab of the Display Properties dialog. Large numbers will appear on each monitor.

set up projector (Mac) p. 110

- Unlike PowerPoint for Windows, you don't need to make any special settings in PowerPoint for the Mac so that it uses a second monitor. The Presenter Tools will appear on the monitor with the menu bar (usually the notebook screen), and the presentation will appear on the projector.

- Most of the time, you don't actually have to turn the computer and projector off before you hook them together. You can connect them, then open the Displays pane of System Preferences. If two display windows don't appear, click the Detect Displays button, which will scan for displays, after which the second display window will appear.

prepare yourself p. 112

- If you want to become a better presenter, there are some terrific online resources. I'm a fan of the Beyond Bullets weblog (www.beyondbullets.com), written by Cliff Atkinson. It's full of practical tips and information that will help you think about using PowerPoint in a different way.

- The best PowerPoint presentation I've ever seen didn't use a single bullet point. It was performed by Scott McCloud, who wrote Understanding Comics (1993, Perennial Currents), a brilliant, essential book that will help you understand all forms of visual communications, including PowerPoint. And it's mostly done as comics! Trust me on this one.

extra bits

run the presentation p. 114

- Besides clicking the mouse or pressing the Right Arrow key, you can also use the following keys to advance slides or perform the next animation: N, Page Down, Enter (Return), Down Arrow, or the spacebar. I usually use the spacebar when I present, because it's the biggest and easiest to find by touch while I'm talking.

- Besides pressing the Left Arrow key, you can also use the following keys to return to the previous slide or return to the previous animation: P, Page Up, Up Arrow, or Delete.

- To jump to a particular slide number, type number and Enter (Return).

- Press B or Period to turn the screen all black; press W or Comma to turn it all white. This is useful if you want to pause for a moment; press the key again to return to the presentation.

- PowerPoint for Mac has the ability to take notes and create action items while you're giving your presentation, using a feature called Meeting Minder. To use it, while your presentation is onscreen, choose Meeting Minder from the Actions pop-up menu at the lower-left corner of the screen.

The Meeting Minder window will appear. You can use it to take minutes or to record action items. If you create action items, they will appear on a new slide at the end of your presentation.

PowerPoint for Windows eliminated the Meeting Minder feature beginning with PowerPoint 2003.

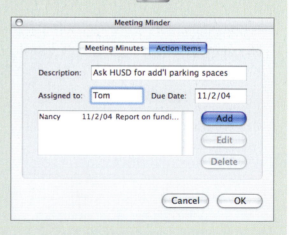

- There are a few great hardware accessories that can help almost any presentation. The first is an inexpensive laser pointer. These are essential for drawing your audience's attention to a part of your slide. I have a fancy (and pricey) laser pointer with a green beam, but that's because I'm a presentation geek. You can find the standard models with red beams for as little as $10. You can also benefit from a remote control for your computer, because they allow you to wirelessly roam anywhere on the stage, rather than being tied to your notebook. These units usually consist of a handheld control and a receiver that connects to your notebook via the USB port. Some of them, such as units from Keyspan (www.keyspan.com) and Targus (www.targus.com), have a built-in laser pointer. If you'll be presenting from a Mac, make sure that the remote is Mac-compatible (most are).

use presenter view p. 116

- On the Mac, you can use the Speaker Notes zoom menu to make the notes larger or smaller, so they are more comfortable to read.

- You can type new notes or change your Speaker Notes during the show on the Mac, but not on Windows. If you have the time while you're presenting, this allows you to incorporate audience feedback during the show.

- Those Previous Slide and Next Slide buttons in Presenter View are nice, but I find that it's easier to click on the much bigger current slide to move forward, or to keep a finger on the spacebar or Right Arrow key on the keyboard.

10. present everywhere

Given the smashing success of your presentation, chances are good that you'll be asked to provide it to others, or take it on the road. As usual, PowerPoint is up to the task. On Windows, you can turn your presentation into a CD that you can send anywhere; on the Mac, you can convert the presentation into a QuickTime movie; and you can even save the show as Web pages that can be viewed by anyone with a Web browser.

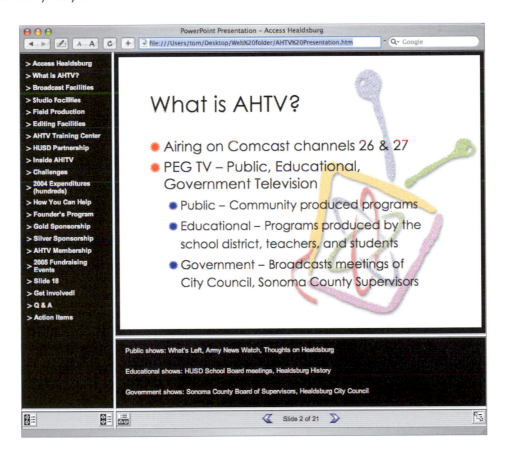

save to CD (Win)

PowerPoint for Windows allows you to turn your presentation into a package, which is a folder or a CD that contains all of the files associated with your presentation, including graphics, the PowerPoint file, fonts, external movies that are linked to the presentation, and sounds. The package will also contain a copy of the PowerPoint Viewer program, so the recipients of the CD don't even have to have PowerPoint installed to admire your work.

The reason why you want to create a package, rather than just copy the presentation file to a CD, is that you need to make sure that all of the elements of your presentation come along with the file. To be efficient and to make sure the PowerPoint presentation file doesn't get too big, PowerPoint will invisibly link large external files (especially video files) into the presentation, but will not copy those files into the presentation file. Similarly, fonts that you have on your system may not be available on another computer, and creating a PowerPoint package will copy the fonts used in the presentation for use by the PowerPoint Viewer.

With your presentation open, choose File > Package for CD. In the resulting dialog, if you don't like the default name of PresentationCD, you can change it.

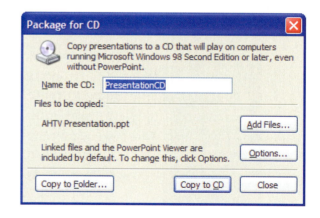

You're not limited to copying only one presentation file to the package; if you want to add additional presentations, click the Add Files button, then use the resulting Add Files dialog to choose the presentation files.

By default, the PowerPoint Viewer and linked external files will be included in the package, and all of the presentations in the package will play automatically when the CD is inserted. To change this, click Options.

present everywhere

If you don't want to include the PowerPoint Viewer, clear that checkbox in the Options dialog. If you want to change how the presentations play in the viewer, select one of the choices in the pop-up menu.

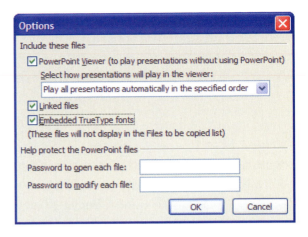

If you don't want to include linked files or embed fonts in the package, clear those checkboxes. Finally, you can optionally enter passwords that will be required to either open or modify the presentation files included in the package. When you're done setting options, click OK. You will return to the Package for CD dialog.

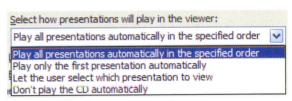

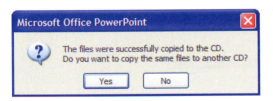

To burn the package to a CD, click Copy to CD. If there isn't a CD already in the drive, PowerPoint will ask you to insert a blank CD. Do so, then click the Retry button. The CD will be burned. Power-Point will ask if you want to make additional CDs. Make your selection.

To save the package as a folder on your hard drive (which you can copy to a networked server, or even burn to a CD later), click Copy to Folder in the Package for CD dialog. In the resulting dialog, give the folder a name and browse to the location on your hard drive where you want to save it.

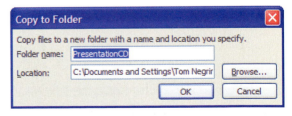

save as movie (Mac)

On the Mac, you can save the presentation as a QuickTime movie, which can be played on any computer that has the QuickTime Player installed (all Macs have this, and QuickTime is often installed on Windows machines). This is PowerPoint for Mac's alternative answer to the PowerPoint Viewer program, but truth be told, it's a poor substitute.

PowerPoint presentations converted to QuickTime movies don't look as good as they do in PowerPoint; text is blocky and line art is noticeably lower in resolution. Worst of all, the resulting movies aren't interactive, which means that slide transitions and effects don't advance when you click the movie or press the Right Arrow key. Because of these fidelity problems, you should think carefully, run tests, and perhaps think about redesigning aspects of your presentation before you distribute it as a QuickTime movie.

To convert a presentation to a QuickTime movie, choose File > Make Movie. The Save dialog will appear. Navigate to where you want to save the movie.

You can change the name of the saved movie in the Save As box. You should adjust the movie settings. To do so, click Movie Options.

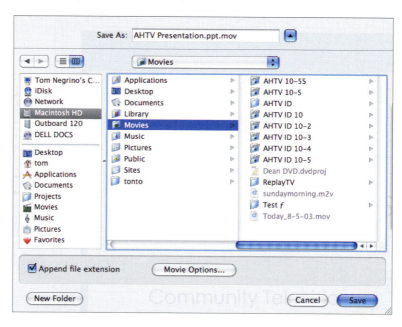

I recommend you use these movie settings: Under Optimization, choose Quality; choose movie dimensions of 640 x 480 (if you are going to edit this movie into other video, click Custom and use 720 x 540); and leave the rest as shown. This will give you a good-quality movie.

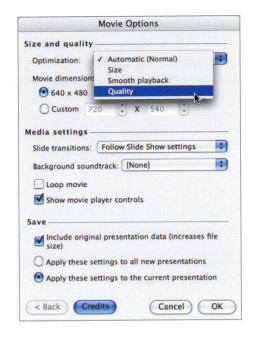

save as a web site

You can make your presentation available to the widest audience by converting it into a Web site and placing it on a Web server, either on the Internet or on your company's intranet. The presentation will be readable by anyone with a Web browser on any major computing platform (Windows, Mac, Linux, and others).

Presentations turned into Web sites resemble Normal View, with the outline on the left, a large area for the slide, and a space for Speaker Notes.

Web presentation from PowerPoint for Windows

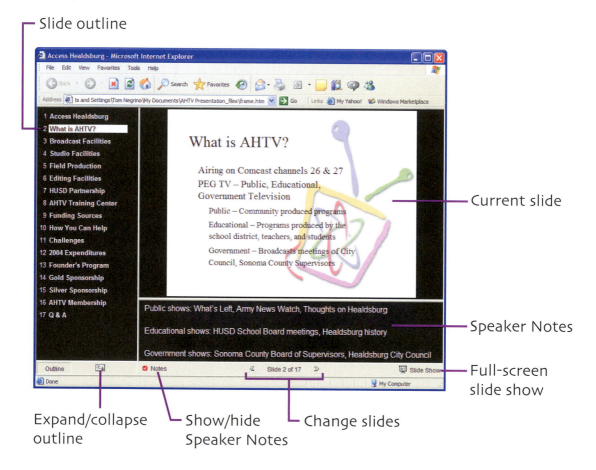

Slide outline

Current slide

Speaker Notes

Full-screen slide show

Expand/collapse outline

Show/hide Speaker Notes

Change slides

present everywhere

Presentations turned into Web sites from PowerPoint for Macintosh look similar to, but are not exactly the same as, presentations converted from PowerPoint for Windows.

Web presentation from PowerPoint for Mac

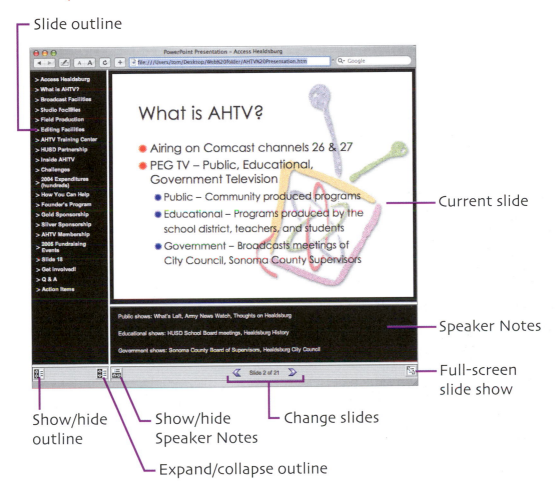

Slide outline

Current slide

Speaker Notes

Full-screen slide show

Show/hide outline

Show/hide Speaker Notes

Change slides

Expand/collapse outline

Besides the differences in the onscreen controls, you can see font differences on the slides, and the presentation converted from the Mac preserved the bullets on the slide, whereas the Windows version did not.

save as a web site (cont.)

To convert your presentation into a Web page, choose File > Save As Web Page. In the Save As dialog (Windows), PowerPoint automatically fills in the file name and the Web page's title with the name of the presentation. You can edit the file name by changing it in the Save As dialog, and the page title by clicking the Change Title button.

If you want to make adjustments to PowerPoint's default settings for Web pages, click Publish. The Publish as Web Page dialog appears, where you can choose whether or not to display your Speaker Notes on the Web. More advanced settings are available by clicking Web Options.

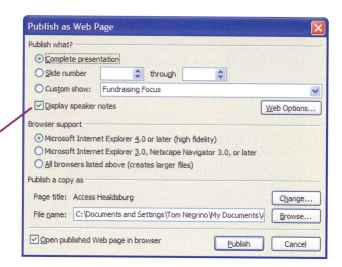

The Mac Save As dialog looks similar.

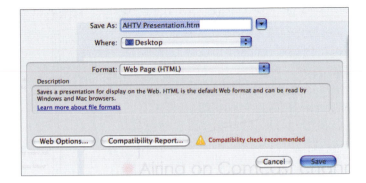

To change the page title or make other adjustments, click Web Options. In the resulting dialog, you can make a variety of useful changes to the look of the exported Web page.

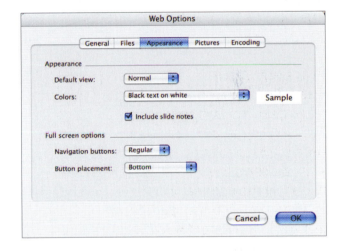

When you're done setting the options, click OK to leave the Web Options dialog, then click Save to save your Web page. The saved Web page will consist of two parts. One is the HTML file, and the other is a companion folder with the files that make up the presentation (text, graphics, etc.).

AHTV Presentation.htm

AHTV Presentation_files

You need to copy the Web page and the companion folder to a Web server for it to be viewable by others. If you don't know how to do that, ask your Web site's administrator.

extra bits

save to CD (Win) p. 124

- If PowerPoint tells you that it isn't able to burn the CD, it may be because your computer has CD-burning software that is incompatible with direct burning from PowerPoint. That doesn't mean that you can't burn a CD with your presentation. The workaround is to save the package as a folder on your hard disk, then use your CD-burning program to copy the folder to a CD.

- Before you save the presentation to a CD, make sure that the presentation's settings are as you want them, especially if you have created Custom Shows. The show selected in Slide Show > Set Up Show will be the one that plays in the Power-Point Viewer.

- Always preview the contents of the CD before you send it off!

- PowerPoint for Mac can save the presentation and associated files as a PowerPoint package, but the package works a little differently than a PowerPoint package on Windows, in that the PowerPoint Viewer program is not included. That's because Microsoft discontinued the PowerPoint Viewer program for Macintosh a few years back. The PowerPoint package on Macintosh is useful when you want to copy your presentation from one disk to another, and you want to make sure that any associated files that might be external to the presentation file (such as large movies or sounds) will be included. To create a PowerPoint package from your presentation on the Mac, choose File > Save As, and then choose PowerPoint Package from the Format pop-up menu in the Save As dialog.

present everywhere

- If you will be creating your presentations using PowerPoint 2004 for Mac and sharing them with Windows users (Power-Point files are largely compatible across platforms), it's a good idea to use the new Compatibility Report feature. This lets you know if your show will have any problems displaying on other (or older) versions of PowerPoint. Choose Tools > Compatibility Report, which opens the associated pane in the Toolbox. If the report shows any problems, you should consider making changes in the presentation.

save as movie (Mac) p. 126

- If there are slide timings in your presentation, the QuickTime movie will use them for the duration of each slide. Most of the time, you'll want the movie to be run manually, meaning that viewers will advance through the presentation on their own. For manual operation, you'll need to clear the slide timings. To do that, switch to Slide Sorter View, and select all the slides in the presentation. Choose Slide Show > Slide Transition, then in the Advance Slide section of the Slide Transition dialog, clear the "Automatically after X seconds" checkbox, and then click Apply to All.

- If you need to install QuickTime for Windows (so you can play a presentation converted to a movie on a Windows machine), you can download the free player from http://www.apple.com/quicktime/download/.

extra bits

- Interestingly, Apple's competing presentation program, Keynote, does a better job of converting presentations to QuickTime movies than PowerPoint does. The movie looks better, plays more smoothly, and is fully interactive, working more like the file would in Keynote or PowerPoint. Keynote also does a very good job of importing PowerPoint files. So if you have Keynote and you need QuickTime movie output, consider first converting your Power-Point file to Keynote, then exporting the Keynote file to a QuickTime movie.

save as a web site p. 128

- If you have upgraded to Windows XP Service Pack 2, you will discover that Internet Explorer objects to viewing your exported PowerPoint presentation. That's because the presentation uses scripting and Active X controls to enhance the viewing experience. Internet Explorer will show the Information Bar, letting you know that the content you are trying to load may be unsafe.

 To help protect your security, Internet Explorer has restricted this file from showing active content that could access your computer. Click here for options... ✕

Of course, your presentation content is OK, so click the word options and choose Allow Blocked Content from the pop-up menu. Your presentation will appear in the Internet Explorer window.

present everywhere

index

index

index

index

Slide Show button, 114
Slide Show View, 8
Slide Sorter button, 82
Slide Sorter View, 8, 45
    rearranging slides in, 82–83, 93
    setting slide transitions in, 84–85, 93
slide text. See text
Slide Transition dialog (Macintosh), 85, 133
Slide Transition Task Pane (Windows), 84,
    93
slide transitions, 81, 84–85, 93
    previewing, 85, 93
    setting, 84–85, 93
Slide View, 8
slides, 9
    designing, 35–46
    entering text on, 14–15, 48
    headers and footers, 11
    hyperlinks to, 58
    printing, 103–104, 106
    rearranging, 82–83, 93
    reorganizing information on, 16–17
    reviewing, 24–25
    viewing layouts of, 26–28, 33
Slides tab, Normal View pane, 2, 24
sound files
    adding, 70, 79
    finding, 31–32
    royalty-free, 33
    supported formats, 79
Sound icon, 70
Sound pop-up menu, 85
SoundRangers, 33
spacebar, 120
Speaker Notes
    creating, 101
    modifying, 121
    printing, 102
    zoom menu, 121
Spelling dialog, 60

Spinner effect, 88–89
spreadsheet data, 80
Standard Toolbar, 6–7
    Macintosh, 4
    Windows, 2
starting PowerPoint, 1
subheadings, 15

T

tables, 76–77, 80
Tables and Borders toolbar, 80
Targus remote control, 121
Task Pane (Windows), 3
    Clip Art pane, 29
    Research pane, 20
    Slide Design options, 36, 44
    Slide Layout options, 26, 38
templates. See design templates
text, 47–62
    aligning, 52, 62
    editing, 48–49
    entering, 14–15, 48
    formatting, 50–51, 61
    hyperlinks in, 56–58, 62
    line breaks in, 48–49
    line spacing in, 53
    numbered lists and, 54–55, 62
    placeholders for, 42–43
    spelling checker for, 60
    text boxes and, 59
    zooming in on, 21
Text and Content Layouts, 27
text boxes, 59
thumbnails, 8, 36, 82
timings
    automatic, 100
    rehearsing, 99–100
Title and Text layout, 15, 39

index

Title layout, 35, 39
Title slide, 14
titles, 9, 130
toolbars
    Diagram, 72
    Drawing, 3, 11
    Formatting, 2, 50–51
    Outlining, 16–17, 18
    Rehearsal, 99
    Standard, 6–7
    Tables and Borders, 80
transitions. See slide transitions
translating words/phrases, 22

U

underlined text, 61
Undo button, 6
Up Next window, 117

V

VGA ports, 108, 110
video clips, 71, 79
    See also movies
View Buttons
    Macintosh, 5
    Windows, 3
viewing
    slide layouts, 26–28, 33
    Web presentations, 128–129
Views, 8
    Normal, 2, 4, 8, 24
    Outline, 8, 13–17
    Presenter, 109, 116–117, 121
    Slide, 8
    Slide Show, 8
    Slide Sorter, 8, 45, 82–85, 93

W

Web Options dialog, 131
Web resources
    for add-in programs, 93
    for clip art, 30, 33
    for graphic editing tools, 45
    for slide templates, 45
    for sounds, 33
Web sites
    adding hyperlinks to, 56–57
    default settings for, 130
    saving presentations as, 128–131, 134
    viewing presentations on, 128–129
Windows Paint program, 45
Windows version of PowerPoint. See
    PowerPoint for Windows
Windows XP Service Pack 2, 134
Wipe effect, 86, 91–92
Word program. See Microsoft Word
writing presentations, 13–22
    entering text, 14–15, 21
    organizing outlines, 16–17, 21
    Research Pane and, 20, 22
    Word program for, 18–19, 22

Z

Zoom menu, 7
    Speaker Notes, 121
    text views, 21